LIVING

Wisely,

LIVING WELL

LIVING
Wisely,

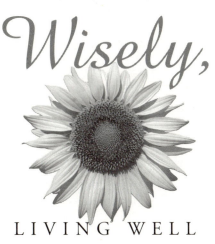

LIVING WELL

Timeless Wisdom to
Enrich Every Day

Swami Kriyananda

crystal clarity **publishers**
nevada city, california

Crystal Clarity Publishers, Nevada City, CA 95959
Copyright © 2010 by Hansa Trust
First edition published 2010.
All rights reserved. Published 2010

Printed in China
ISBN-13: 978-1-56589-261-3
ePub ISBN: 978-1-56589-633-8

Cover and Interior layout and design by Tejindra Scott Tully

Library of Congress Cataloging-in-Publication Data

Kriyananda, Swami.
  Living wisely, living well : timeless wisdom to enrich every day /
Swami Kriyananda. — 1st ed.
    p. cm.
  Rev. ed. of: Do it well! : timeless wisdom to enrich every day. 1st ed.
  ISBN 978-1-56589-261-3
  1. Self-actualization (Psychology) 2. Conduct of life. I. Kriyananda,
Swami. Do it well! II. Title.

  BF637.S4.K75 2010
  294.5'432—dc22

                                2010019417

www.crystalclarity.com
clarity@crystalclarity.com
800-424-1055

Preface

Have you ever felt bewildered when facing a difficult decision in your life? A good friend who is at a personal crossroads recently said to me, "I wish God would just appear and tell me what to do!"

How often we've all had similar thoughts, only to flounder for lack of clear direction. But God *does* tell us what to do. He speaks to us more often than we realize, often in the form of wise, impartial friends. Swami Kriyananda, through the sayings in this book, is such a friend.

Having had the privilege of knowing him for over forty years, I've observed that Swamiji himself has faithfully practiced the precepts he recommends in this book. In the vernacular, he "walks his talk."

Through his practice, Kriyananda has mastered the art of living. His profound, loving insights, gleaned from a lifetime of seeking truth, offer the guidance we need to be *living wisely and well* with confidence and faith.

–Nayaswami Devi

Introduction

The sayings in this book consist of lessons I myself have learned in life, whether by experience or through trial and error; sometimes by deep pain or disappointment; many times through an inner joy almost unbearable. Someone said to me many years ago, "*You* can write happy songs; you've never suffered." I replied, "On the contrary, it's because I *have* suffered that I've earned the right to express happiness." What I've presented here is the fruit of many years of thoughtfully directed living.

This represents a complete revision of a former book of mine, *Do It NOW!* Of the more than one hundred books I have written so far in my life, *Do It NOW!* was always (until now, that is) one of my favorites—so much so, in fact, that when I first published it in 1995 I actually, in my eagerness to share it with others, paid the printing costs myself for five thousand copies, which I gave away freely to others.

Today, fourteen years later, I offer this revised version both because of my continued enthusiasm for the book, and out of my continued growth in the insights it expresses. I ask you, *as a favor to yourself*: Buy, beg, or borrow this collection of *pensées*. (But don't steal it!—see the saying for April 10.) Keep it on your nightstand or in your meditation room. Read from it every morning, and ponder, throughout the day, the thoughts expressed. If even one saying should spare you some of the pains I have experienced in my own life, I shall feel amply rewarded. For whatever tests you face or have faced, they will very likely resemble some that I, too, have known.

Resolve difficulties by raising your level of consciousness. Keep your mind focused at the point midway between the eyebrows: the seat of superconsciousness.

Smile with your eyes, not only with your lips.

When communicating face to face with others, express your thoughts also through your eyes. To rely only on words is to reduce communication by half.

Your *reactions* to events are more important in your life than the events themselves. Make sure that you react always in such a way as to increase your inner peace and happiness.

When conversing with people, try always to talk *with* them, not merely *at* them.

When laughing, laugh from your heart. There is no joy in intellectual laughter. Indeed, such laughter often becomes only a snicker of disdain.

In any controversy, test the rightness of your stand by the way it affects your deeper feelings. Such feelings can be trusted, as the ever-fickle emotions can never be. Calm, joyful feelings will steer you aright. If, on the other hand, your feelings are agitated or negative, they will emphasize your lower emotions, and will almost always be wrong. Even happy emotions can distort one's judgment. Calm feeling is the safest condition for receiving right guidance.

Assuming that you really do want others to listen to you, show them the respect of listening to them first—of hearing what they have to say. Even if they say nothing, listen first.

Listen to the melodies birds sing: They express a happiness that is latent everywhere in Nature. Reflect then: You, too, are a part of that happiness. It is the first little "cheep" of omnipresent joy.

Watch your reactions to others. If you see in anyone some quality that attracts you, try to develop it in yourself. But if you see a quality that to you is displeasing, then, instead of criticizing it, work to expunge it from your personality. Remember, the world will only mirror back to you what you are in yourself.

Listen to the subtle undertones in your voice. Ask yourself why people's voices express so much variety. The mechanism of speech never changes. One might expect its tones to be as alike as trumpets! Yet each voice has intonations that are uniquely its own. An American once, at the airport in Patna, India, recognized me solely by my voice. He hadn't seen me for fifteen years, when I'd been a teenager in high school; he had no idea that I was even in India. Listen, therefore, to your own voice. Try to expunge from it any qualities you don't like. Sweeten it with kindness; brighten it with interest; soften it by heartfelt respect for others; warm it with consideration for their needs.

JANUARY 12

To inject warmth into your voice, relax it physically, then project interest, and your concern for others' well-being, outward to them. Let your voice rise from the heart, flow smoothly through the vocal cords (never tensely, as if forcing itself through fierce opposition!), then outward through your spiritual eye at a point midway between the eyebrows.

JANUARY 13

Talk *meaningfully*. Never chatter as if merely to let people know that you are present, and would like to be accounted for! Watch your words carefully; give them the luster of intelligence, even when speaking in fun.

If you find yourself becoming agitated, relax the feeling quality in your heart. There, in what appears to be only a physical organ, lies the origin of all feelings, whether excited or calm. The feeling quality is the essence of consciousness. Without that, one would be a mere mechanism—as materialists, in fact, insist we all are. Their dogma teaches that clear understanding demands the elimination of all feelings. That dogma is fatally flawed. Without both feeling and self-awareness, there could be no life! The whole universe is a projection of the Supreme Self, in Whom lies also the perfection of feeling: Absolute Bliss. Two things science will never be able to create: feeling of any kind, and self-awareness.

Practice living with greater awareness. Let your energy flow out to others from your heart—first to those whom you know, and then, by degrees, to the whole world. Let your impact on others always be beneficial.

Cultivate the art of brevity. A single well-phrased sentence will be long remembered, whereas long discourses are usually soon forgotten. In writing this book, too, I have tried to make every sentence as short and concise as possible. Meandering sentences often lose themselves, like country paths, in the unkempt grass of tangled thinking.

Look for qualities to appreciate in others. What you see in them is a reflection of what you are in yourself. The more you appreciate others, the more they will return that feeling—like the strings of a musical instrument, which vibrate in sympathy with kindred notes elsewhere. But if you see qualities in others that you dislike, your negative reaction will be a sign that you have the same unattractive qualities in yourself. Use your negative opinions of others, in this case, as goads to self-transformation.

Choose your words with kindness, inviting receptivity and understanding. Think of what you might say that will *help* others, and not merely stimulate them.

If rumor has preceded you, you might tell people, "Rumor is a beast with many heads, and with as many tongues. It may be wisest to let your own experience of me show you to which head you should listen."

Think time and space when you speak. Give others the time they need to absorb your ideas, and the space to enlarge on their own.

If you really want to communicate with others, seek also to *commune* with them. *Feel* their consciousness. Appreciate them for what they are and for what they do, not only for what they say.

To make your thoughts interesting, infuse melody into your speech. A flat voice suggests a flat personality. If you yourself are interested in what you are saying, let your voice express that interest. Don't use words as mere beasts of burden for your ideas. Automatically, if you (in a sense) sing your words, your voice will gain in cadence, color, and rhythm.

Laugh *with* others, but never *at* them. Let them feel that you are their friend. Avoid the boisterous laughter that is so commonly heard at revels. When I say laugh with others, I refer to that softer, more intimate sound which comes with inner appreciation for their company.

Listen for the unexpressed thoughts and feelings behind what people say. Often their words will only mask their real intentions. A common tendency when speaking is first to "test the water," to see if it is warm enough for swimming.

The secret of earthly happiness is to flow gracefully with change. Allow things freely to come and go. All things pass: people, events, time—life itself. Learn to accept every fresh experience joyfully.

Get rid of likes and dislikes. They only agitate the mind, and prevent one from seeing things as they really are. Instead, practice inner contentment (*santosha*, in Sanskrit).

For clarity, edit at least mentally what you say or write—always placing emphasis on simplicity, directness, and rhythm. Convoluted sentences merely bewilder the mind. Clarity requires special attention: Try to think *with* others. Take into account also their varied levels of understanding.

Say only what you mean. In your most casual speech be sincere, and you'll find others listening to you instead of gazing off in furtive search of a clock.

Concentrate on your present commitments; don't dwell regretfully on past failures. Your life will keep on improving if, *at this very moment*, you do your very best.

In communicating with others, don't speak only from your intellect: speak from your heart. Many problems would be resolved if people would learn the right balance between head and heart. The need to balance these two is the psychological reason for the attraction between the sexes.

Live in the present moment: Enjoy it; learn from it. As the years pass, you'll not only develop golden memories, but will find it easier to develop *smriti* (divine memory), the classic definition of enlightenment.

If someone challenges something you are doing that seems to you right and good, meet that challenge vigorously. Try never to hurt anyone, however; be always calm in your heart. Remember, nothing and no one can touch who you really are, in your inner Self.

Think of time as a radiation outward from your own center. Past and future move not only directionally like a river: they also revolve around their center in the changeless NOW.

If someone impugns you or your honor (in the sense of attacking your "good name" or reputation) ignore him. If that isn't possible, seek a graceful, even a humorous way out—like the American in France who once met a Frenchman's challenge to a duel by selecting, for weapons, "apple pie at ten paces." After all, what is that false "honor" but an affirmation of ego: the root cause of all suffering?! Suffice it if you, following your own conscience, act honorably. People's unflattering opinions of you are not your problem, but theirs.

Give people the time they need to express themselves clearly. The rhythms of thought vary, but sincere self-expression requires careful, and sometimes prolonged, deliberation.

Mental attitudes are often reflected in bodily positions. Do you lean habitually forward, as if to grasp at events before they happen? Do you lean backward, as if to distance yourself from others or from some unpleasantness? Do you tend to lean sideways, as if to find a strategy for getting around some obstacle? Keep your bodily and mental posture upright, relaxed, and serene. You'll find it relatively easy, then, to cope with any difficulties that confront you.

Your body is a temple more truly than any edifice built by hands. Enter therein daily. Move in solemn procession up the aisle of the spine to God's high altar in the forehead (the seat of superconscious ecstasy). Worship God at that altar in the spiritual eye.

Keep in your heart a constant, flowing conversation with God. Address Him in the second person as "You," not as "He" or "She," nor even in the nowadays-stilted form, "Thou." Share with Him or Her—your Cosmic Friend— every thought, every feeling of your heart.

Respect everyone, even if some people strike you as a bit daft. Remember, God dwells in all beings, and can express His wisdom in countless ways—sometimes quite surprisingly. I myself have found that, when I listened open-mindedly to someone whom I thought a little foolish, it was that person, specifically, whom God chose to tell me something I needed to hear.

Never lend money unless you can feel, in your heart, that you are giving the money away. This practice will spare you much pain. For as Shakespeare (through Polonius) said, "Loan oft loseth both itself and friend." Tell God that you place the money in His hands. He will see to it that you don't lack in consequence. Be sensible, however, in your lending. Try to ensure that the help you give goes to someone whose need is real. Reflect on those movie actors who carelessly gave away large amounts of the money they were earning, but who years later died in penury.

Avoid negative thinking. Remember, whatever you project outward to the world will return to you. A boomerang effect is inevitable.

To be fully aware, look for the hidden reality behind all appearances.

If someone insults or makes fun of you, thank him (even warmly) and say, "I appreciate your reminder that I'm very far from perfect. Since perfection is what I hope to attain someday, I consider it a helpful reminder to be told I still have work to do."

State the truth in a normal, conversational tone. Often, people who shout their thoughts are either lying or talking through their hats.

Live more in the heart. Send rays of love out to all the world, knowing that everyone aspires, each in his own way, to the highest possible attainment: perfect bliss. Bliss, in union with God, must come eventually to everyone.

If anything or anyone distresses you, think how you'll probably feel a week—a month—a year later. If you can imagine yourself being happy and peaceful then, why waste all that time? Be happy and peaceful *now*!

Treat others as though it were a treat to be with them!

Listen for expressions of truth in the simple speech of children. See what you can learn from them. Their insights are less conditioned by convention, and often are refreshingly perceptive. Be careful, however, not to be so childlike as to create trouble for others. To give an amusing but illustrative example, during my family's visit to America when I was nine, my mother took us three boys across the border into Canada. As we returned through customs, the officer asked her, "Have you anything to declare?" "Nothing," she replied. Instantly all three of us, hands over our mouths, cried out, "Oh, Mother!" Sternly, the official ordered her to open the trunk. There he found three little birchbark canoes, six inches long. So—be childlike, but don't be naive!

Speak the truth kindly: never in a judgmental spirit, and never sarcastically. Speak it to be helpful, not to destroy another person's self-confidence.

When setting out to accomplish anything, give less thought to what has already been done than to what is required of this particular task, at this particular moment.

Encourage others in their efforts to improve themselves. But remember, *they don't owe it to you* to be better than they are. That debt is one they owe only to themselves.

Be patient with people. Remember, it takes incarnations to emerge from the pit of delusion. Think how long it probably took *you* to reach your present level of understanding, and how long it often takes to rid oneself of even one major flaw.

Bring peace first to your own heart, then send it out on gentle rays of light to all the world. The more you radiate your peace outward, the more you'll find yourself protected from all harm.

FEBRUARY 23

Treat your friends as though you had much to learn from them. There is no surer way of losing a friend than to let him feel you need nothing from him.

FEBRUARY 24

Think of this day as a friend. God gave it to you; He wants you to be happy in it. If it rains, tell yourself, "God wants to cleanse me, through this downpour, of all impurities." And if the sun shines, think of its warmth as God's encouragement to you to do your best in everything.

33

When teaching or advising others, feel that you are only *sharing* with them your ideas, your knowledge, and your experience. Never be condescending or didactic.

A key to introspection is to focus on the rhythms of your breath: on its calmness or rapidity; on its force of flow; on the location of that flow in the nostrils; on each pause between the breaths; on the relative length of inhalation to exhalation (in sleep, for instance, exhalation is twice as long as inhalation). Your breathing is a reflection of your mental state. As you watch it, you will find yourself becoming inwardly calm, and your stillness, in turn, will deepen your introspection.

State your opinions impersonally, but not too forcefully lest you draw attention more to yourself than to your ideas. Where deep conviction is concerned, however, speak also with the vigor of commitment.

To overcome nervousness while teaching or lecturing, concentrate on *giving out* to people rather than on making a good impression.

To overcome fear of misjudgment by others, think of (and speak to) them kindly. Your fears will then move from self-concern to an expansive interest in their well-being.

View life as a mountain to be climbed, each upward step a move closer to the top, and to perfection. Welcome any difficulties you encounter on the way. Each time you face a test bravely, your strength will increase. Concentrate on what is required of you at each step of the way, for you to reach the summit.

Respect others, and they will always respect you. Despise them, and they'll find many ways to express their contempt.

After every deed that you perform, pause a little to enjoy the freedom of the Self within. Action, to be fully effective, must proceed from inner calmness.

Act without desire for the fruits of your action. Take care of the present, and the future will take care of itself. The past will then cease to be a burden on your conscience, and the future will await you with a smile.

If you want loyalty from others, give them your loyalty first. Loyalty to friends, to ideals, to commitments is like a rudder: it holds the barque of life true to its course.

More important even than love, in your behavior toward others, are your respect and loyalty. In love there may be attachment or desire, but in respect and loyalty there is only self-giving.

Gaze into the sun when it is near the horizon. (Its rays, then, will not harm your eyes.) God, through the sun, sends out rays of power, endurance, and wisdom. In India, certain yogis practice gazing into the sun, and claim they receive therefrom wise insight and inspiration.

If someone tells lies about you, respond calmly, with dignity. If a comment is required of you, you might say, "My critic has missed his mark this time, but is it an issue that I'm imperfect? The perfection I seek is a blessing I wish for him also, and for everyone."

Be courteous equally to friends, foes, and strangers. Courtesy will win you respect and cooperation, and courtesy to friends will preserve that slight distance between you which keeps friendship ever fresh, alive, and interesting.

Gaze into the moon, especially at the full. Feel in its rays the Divine Mother's eternal love for you, and for all Her human children.

Listen as much to the tone of people's voices as to their words. *How* they speak often expresses as much as *what* they say.

Hold kindness in your heart for every-one. Blame nobody for the mistakes he commits. Reflect: All human beings are struggling to find their own way out of the jungle of delusion.

To become inwardly free, live to serve others rather than for personal gain. Service is magnanimity, and the prerogative of kings. But the more you work for personal gain, the more you will only beggar yourself.

Answer rudeness with courtesy. You might reply with a smile, "Life is all the richer for the many points of view it presents."

Treat differences of opinion respectfully. You may then find agreement between what, at first, looked like two irreconcilable points of view.

The more you share with others, the more you will receive in life the blessing of abundance.

How should you respond to a false accusation? You might try answering, "Now that you've reduced me to a level you can handle, may we talk as friends?" (That subtle reprimand will be well deserved!)

In addressing those who have spoken against you, say to them, "Thank you. You've helped me affirm that which alone is real to me: the joy of my own being." A "friend" once spent more than one hour coldly denouncing me for all the faults he had perceived in me. They seemed in some way to disturb his peace of mind. I listened in silence, then thanked him. There was nothing more to be

said. After his departure, however, I wrote what I think
of as one of my best songs, the lyrics of which go:

> *Though green summer fade*
> *And winter draw near,*
> *My Lord, in Your presence*
> *I live without fear.*

> *Through tempest, through snows,*
> *Through turbulent tide,*
> *The touch of Your hand*
> *Is my strength, and my guide.*

> *I ask for no riches*
> *That death can destroy.*
> *I crave only Thee:*
> *Your love, and Your joy.*

> *The dancers will pass;*
> *The singing must end:*
> *I welcome the darkness*
> *With You for my Friend.*

For this song I am forever grateful to my self-styled enemy
and ill-wisher.

Even when threatened by disaster, if you are steadfastly honest and truthful you will not only survive: you will flourish.

Make it a point, today, to laugh at least three times from your heart. Such laughter is the strongest antidote for disease, depression, and corroding sorrow of every kind.

Criticize no one. If you must offer correction, give that person a way to preserve his self-respect. When others feel your support, they will support you in turn—perhaps at times when you need it most.

Trust life, even if you cannot trust people. For human nature is unreliable, but life itself is ruled by immutable law. Right action leads always, in the end, to victory.

Try always to relate to what *is*, not to what you wish were so.

Today, treat as a friend some neighbor whom you scarcely know. Ask him what you might do to make the nearness of your residences more pleasing to him. By your good will, contradict the ancient dictum, "Your neighbor is your enemy; your neighbor's neighbor is your friend."

Try to understand points of view that are different from your own. The mind, like the body, must be stretched now and then to keep it limber, lest it ossify.

When bargaining, seek benefits that are mutual. If you express yourself generously, the other person will usually, of his own accord, meet you halfway.

Never impose an idea on anyone. *Offer* it kindly, as a suggestion for his consideration. You'll find him readier, then, to accept it.

Life asks of us many compromises.
Make sure only that you adapt the compromises to your principles, and never your principles to any compromise.

Don't try to impress others with your cleverness. Win them, rather, by your sincerity.

Think of your life as dancing on air. In spirit, soar up on gossamer wings of pure joy. Brush lightly by every mountain peak of difficulty.

Counting to ten is a well-known technique for dissipating anger. You might carry this practice a step further: Visualize, with each number you count, a progressive expansion of awareness. Your perspective will thereby broaden incrementally, dissipating your anger, and changing your whole outlook—first to acceptance, then to empathetic understanding.

Humor arises out of a sudden release of tension with the introduction of some unexpected incongruity. This release, if followed by an *upward* relaxation into the higher Self, may give a fleeting glimpse of soul-joy. Let this year's "April Fool's Day," then, bring you upward release into the happiness of your inner being, and not draw you down into whirlpools of mockery and cynicism.

Generosity in victory is *self*-conquest. It loosens the shackles of pride, and fills one with a deep sense of inner gratitude.

If you have a good idea, it may be "the better part of valor" to discuss it with those only who share your *ideals*. Protect it from people who might jeer, simply because it fails to conform with their preconceptions. Let your confidence gain strength before exposing the idea to human goats, who take pleasure in nibbling on other people's inspirations.

Attachments are self-limiting—like prison bars. Ah, but see! Between the bars there is space. If you concentrate on that space, the bars will disappear: they consist only of your own "iron" stubbornness, its atoms being your repeated affirmation of a false reality.

◈ **APRIL 5** *◈*

To achieve inner freedom, make a mental bonfire every night, before you go to sleep, of all your attachments, self-definitions, desires, and aversions. Nothing that can be measured, weighed, timed, or hoarded can ever truly belong to you. Toss into the flames, piece by piece, every obstacle to your inner peace. Feel your joy soaring skyward, as your limitations, one by one, go up in smoke.

◈ **APRIL 6** *◈*

Make it a point today to tell someone whom you love, "I deeply appreciate you for what you *are*, for what you have done for others, and for what you have given me." Never take anyone close to you for granted.

Make it a point this day to single out someone whose worth many have failed to appreciate. Take the time to show him or her your appreciation. (That person must, after all, have *some* admirable quality! Emphasize it.)

Welcome any suggestion for improving your ideas. At the same time, protect them from others' meddling. Be clear in your mind as to your true intentions.

Purity, innocence, and an absence of selfish motive: these, together, form a diadem more brilliant than that displayed on any emperor's brow.

Let nothing tempt you ever to compromise an ideal. Morality is not a question of convention. The Ten Commandments are engraved in human nature on tablets of light. The true reason why theft, violence, murder, and other crimes are wrong is that they hurt first of all the perpetrator himself, condemning him to ever-deeper dungeon levels in the rock fortress of his egoism. If you arm yourself, however, with truthfulness, honesty, and integrity, you will emerge someday into perfect soul-freedom.

APRIL 11

Tune into others' inner realities. Though the words you speak be similar, your realities may be as different as unrelated languages.

Be more concerned with understanding others than with being understood by them. They too, then, will usually give you their support.

Be "solution-oriented," not "problem-oriented." Problem-consciousness only draws to itself more problems, as flypaper draws flies. But solution-consciousness, like a magnet, attracts answers and shines a bright light onto every difficulty.

Be happy in yourself. If, in a plea for happiness, you hold out a begging bowl to life, the bowl will remain always empty.

APRIL 15

Don't confuse intelligence with cleverness. True intelligence isn't only cerebral. Its roots lie in clear feeling. Cleverness usually indicates only narrow feelings.

APRIL 16

See every problem as an opportunity. Whenever you demolish the obstacles before you, your power for ultimate victory will increase.

APRIL 17

Be restful in your heart. A quiet spirit will help you instantly to resolve problems that might otherwise require days, weeks, or even months of fretful pondering—and even then you wouldn't be certain of the rightness of your decision.

Speak kindly to animals. As human beings are helped upward in their evolution by keeping saintly company, so animal evolution is hastened by association with human beings. You yourself will be helped also, if you extend a helping hand to creatures lower than yourself on the evolutionary scale.

Seek upliftment in the company you keep. Others' magnetism will affect you, whether for good or evil. Make it a point to mix more with people who radiate goodness. Live, if possible, with spiritually minded people. Especially, seek out and live in a community whose members are dedicated to living by high principles.

In any magnetic interchange, what you give out to others will affect what you receive from them. To ensure the greatest protection from all harmful influences, try to act as a channel of divine blessings to all.

Eat either alone or in uplifting company. When one is eating, he places himself in a frame of mind to absorb energy. He is then more open than usual to the vibrations around him. In public eating places, the vibrations are heterogeneous. There, be centered more than usually in the spine. Otherwise, visit such places with true friends. And always eat in harmony.

APRIL 22

Gaze into the eyes of people whose magnetism you'd like to attract. Avoid, on the other hand, the gaze of those whose magnetism might adversely affect your inner peace. Your eternal duty in life is to emerge from the swamp of ignorance, which breeds the pestilence of suffering. Avoid contact with anyone whose magnetism might draw you downward. Delusion keeps people in error for countless incarnations; it has its own dark magnetism. Those who seek truth must avoid ignorance as they would a contagious disease. Avoid especially the brooding gaze of those who live only to gratify their senses.

APRIL 23

Don't ask more of others than you would ask of yourself.

The vibratory interchange between the sexes generates a strong magnetism. Maintain, therefore, a discreet mental distance from, and minimize your contact with, those of the other sex whose consciousness is sensual or worldly. As much as possible, avoid contact of the eyes or hands. (A handclasp creates two horseshoe magnets: the one upward, uniting the upper bodies; the other downward, uniting the lower.) With such people, take care to be centered in the Self.

A principle of magnetic interchange between people is that the stronger magnet always influences the weaker, never the reverse. Unless your inner strength is great, never think yourself capable of uplifting others merely by the exercise of good will.

Keep a spiritual bodyguard, especially when circumstances require you to mix with uncongenial people. The magnetism of two is stronger than that of one. When moving in a crowd, try never to go alone; always have a few friends around you. If you must be in crowds, imagine yourself haloed by an aura of light. Consciously emanate vibrations of love and joy all around you. One evening, years ago, I was obliged to enter the nightclub district of San Francisco. As I went, I silently chanted, *"Sri Ram, jai Ram, jai jai Ram."* I was aware of tentacles of negativity reaching out to grab me, but they slipped by without even touching me.

Sow seeds of faith, where others have sown doubt.

Be grateful always—to others, to life, to God. Express appreciation for everything. Appreciation and gratitude—even for such tests as suffering—will attract to you the blessing of increasing abundance.

Let others feel your support in their worthwhile undertakings. Even if they do something of which you don't approve, let them feel your support for what they *are*.

To break a person's will is a sin before God. Allow others to develop at their own pace, to make their own mistakes, to learn their own lessons. How else will they ever evolve, spiritually?

Sound and light affect our consciousness, for we (like them) are composed of vibrations. Music therefore is more than entertainment, and lighting, more than something to see by. Sound and light actually affect our consciousness, and help direct it toward spirituality, worldliness, or depravity. Be sensitive to the subtle effect of vibrations. Protect yourself from disruptive ones by listening to inspiring music, or by singing (even mentally) songs that are uplifting, and by surrounding yourself with calm, soothing, or brightly cheerful lights and colors.

There are two kinds of innocence: that of ignorance, and that of wisdom. A little girl, asked once by a little boy, "Are you a virgin?" replied, "No; not yet." Hers was the innocence of ignorance. Such innocence may in time be undermined. The innocence of wisdom, however, follows upon the complete conquest of ego. Such innocence, though childlike, can never be undone. Its strength, though flexible, is indomitable.

True happiness is not the fruit of years of painful struggle and anxiety. It is a long succession, rather, of little decisions simply to *be* happy in the moment. As my Guru said, "The minutes are more important than the years."

Select music for its pleasing or uplifting melody, rhythm, and harmony. A melody can do more than entertain: it can uplift; it can fill you with longing; or, alternatively, it can depress you. A rhythm can calm, invigorate, or disturb the nervous system. Harmony can evoke deep, calm feelings of peace, love, and happiness, or incite to anger, haunt with loneliness, torment with anxiety. Choose your music wisely, for its influence on you can be deep. A woman once tried to commit suicide. She had a near-death experience in which she found herself in a hellish region where the vibrations, as she reported later, were very similar to the beat of heavy rock 'n' roll music. Later, she devoted her life to warning people against the insidious influence of such self-lowering music.

The colors of the rainbow have not only a visual impact. They can also affect you vibrationally, when they resonate with the field of energy surrounding you—that is to say, your aura. Surround yourself with pure colors. Muddy hues can obscure mental clarity. Bright hues can induce brighter emotions. Colors should resonate with your nature as it is, and with the qualities you would like to develop in yourself.

The color red can be cheerful. It can also—especially if it is muddy—stimulate to lust or anger. If red resonates with you, make sure that it affects you in the right way, by making you brighter, more cheerful, happier.

The color orange suggests fire. It helps one to generate enthusiasm for destroying all desires and attachments. It can also be irritating, however, especially if one tends toward placidity. And orange can feed a tendency to cry out to people, "Look at me!" Think of workers on the roads. They purposely wear orange to be noticed, so that cars won't hit them.

Yellow is the color of wisdom, insight, and calm acceptance. This color can also, however, be disturbing for those who shrink from meeting challenges. If what you seek in life is progress, yellow may help you to become more creative. An impure yellow, however, can have a somewhat sickening effect on the mind.

Green is the color of health and harmony; it is most visible among growing things. Green gives a heightened sense of physical and mental well-being. Where there is a focus on health, however, there can also be one on ill health. Unpleasant shades of green can disturb the feelings. Green, therefore, is associated also with harmful emotions such as envy and jealousy.

Blue is the color of expansive calmness. If it lacks warmth, however, its effect on the feelings can be chilling. (Think of the expression, "steely blue.") This color, therefore, should also be given a touch of warmth to keep its influence uplifting and devotional. Blue is a good color for meditation.

Indigo implies pure feelings, and the love of beauty in all its manifestations. Choose this color to deepen your love for others, and for God, as well as your appreciation for everything good in life. Indigo has its negative aspects, however, especially for those whose emotions take them downward. Don't let indigo generate in you attitudes of rejection or withdrawal.

Violet is the color of high thoughts, high prin-ciples, noble aspirations. This color will help you to rise out of the lower emotions into the realization that you, in your true Self, are pure Spirit. Violet in its negative aspects can erect a psychic wall between yourself and the earthly realities around you, making your ideals unreal-istic and impractical.

White is a blend of all the colors of the rainbow. If the energy moves up the spine toward the brain, white can inspire a consciousness of purity. If that energy withdraws passively into the spine, however, white may suggest a bland lack of interest. Choose white to develop non-attachment to worldliness. Don't choose it if your nature is too passive.

Ideas should be presented with simple, grounding examples. Try never to offer mere abstractions. The more specific you can be, the clearer your concepts will be to yourself, and the clearer also the understanding you convey to others. When describing waves on a vast ocean, for example, first see them clearly in your mind. Hear them; *feel* them. That clear visualization will help you to make your presentation more vivid.

Make inner freedom your primary goal in life. See every binding desire or attachment as a rope tying your balloon of consciousness to the ground. Sever those ropes, and exclaim vigorously with each slash, "You can hold me no longer! My place is high in the sky, soaring over seas and continents on breezes of pure bliss."

Every time you inhale, imagine yourself inhaling energy. *Pranayama* (a yoga practice) means not only "breath control," but "control of energy." As air fills your lungs, feel your entire being— body, mind, feelings, aspirations—swelling with energy and joy.

Eat a balanced diet. A good formula for doing so is to select foods that are varied in color: the deeper the color, usually, the richer their energy.

When presenting your ideas, illustrate them with familiar examples. The closer to home, the easier they will be to understand. Children, for example, are often told the pleasant myth that there is a pot of gold at the end of every rainbow. Show them how to test the truth of this claim. Suggest they dig at the end of the rainbow which appears in the spray of a garden sprinkler. Could there really be gold there? Tell them, "Dig there and see for yourselves."

Advice for men: If you maintain a certain reserve in the presence of women, they will always respect you.

Advice for women: There are two very different ways of relating to men. Flirtation is an easy way of winning them, and success may give you a sense of power over them. That power is delusive, however. Men will subconsciously resent you for drawing on their energy, even if they aren't sensitive enough to understand the reason for their resentment. If your behavior toward them is more self-giving—like that of a mother, or a friend—you will *increase* their energy, and they will always appreciate you. This is why women in India are spoken of as men's *shakti* (strength, or energy). As temptresses, however, they are not *shakti*, but *ashakti*.

Advice, again, for men: It is easier for you to be impersonal. Therefore, in your search for God, dwell more on thoughts of infinity, of freedom from ego, of desire for the well-being of all. Let your search be more for His Bliss than for His love. Think in terms of serving others self-expansively.

Further advice for women: Because it comes more naturally to you to be personal, concentrate on developing an intimate, I-and-Thou relationship with God. Serve Him in personal ways. Create a beautiful altar; surround yourself with inspiring spiritual images. Enjoy Nature's beauties as God's gift to you, personally.

Advice to men on the subject of balance:

As men progress spiritually, they acquire certain feminine characteristics, becoming softer, gentler, more sensitively aware of others' needs, and more willing to listen sympathetically to what others have to say (these being signs of feminine maturity, though many women exist who need still to mature in these respects!). The reason breasts are attractive is that they suggest tenderness of heart. Physically speaking, men too may, for this reason, develop slight breasts, and the sensitivity in them of a young girl entering puberty. At this point it may become difficult for men to conceal their softer feelings: they may weep easily.

Advice to women seeking balance: As you progress spiritually, your feminine nature will become balanced by masculine characteristics. You will find yourself becoming more affirmative; less personal; firmer in your step; more outwardly expressive as your energy becomes centered more at the point between the eyebrows. Your every gesture, then, will be more decisive.

In balance: The natural attraction between the sexes ceases to be compelling, and becomes merely a subject of interest. Men cease to feel obliterated by women. (Notice, at mixed parties, how often the men present remain silent). Women, in turn, cease to feel individually bullied by men. Men stop (in a positive way) feeling tenderly protective of women, and women stop depending on men for protection. Both sexes appear to each other as human beings, simply, equal in worth like the two sides of a coin.

Accept adversity calmly. In the cosmic drama, adversity is inevitable. Indeed, without tension there would be *no* drama. But the greatest trials can be turned to advantage if they are accepted calmly.

Don't joke too much, lest you trivialize your relationships. Controlled merriment helps to release tension, but unrestrained jocularity keeps the mind light, and is a hindrance to deep thought.

Live more within yourself. Always remain a little reserved, even when laughing. Be soft-spoken, respectful, and appreciative of everyone and everything. When you are alone, remain centered in the Self.

Think how many kinds of laughter there are!
The "belly laugh" which proceeds from excessive body- and matter-consciousness. The gentle laugh that emanates from the cervical center behind the throat, and conveys a sense of calmness. Laughter that originates in the medulla oblongata (at the base of the brain), affirms ego-consciousness. Laughter that emanates from the Christ center between the eyebrows suggests clear discernment. When laughter suggests energy moving downward in the spine, it tends to be cynical, bitter, or sarcastic. The best laughter of all is that which directs energy upward from the heart to the brain, then becoming focused at the Christ center between the eyebrows.

If someone criticizes you, answer him, "I appreciate your advice, and will think about it." Thus, you will not necessarily be saying that you agree with him, but you will show yourself open to improvement. Never let anyone put you on the defensive.

Forgive others, and life itself will forgive you. Any karmic blows you attract, then, will be deflected, or at least softened, by a protective aura.

Speak the truth always, but kindly and impersonally. To call someone ugly or stupid might be a fact, but it will be essentially untrue, for divine wisdom and beauty underlie all outer manifestations. Try always to speak the helpful truth.

Truthfulness requires an acceptance of things as they are. Wishful thinking leads to wishful talking, which can bend perception to suit one's own, and others', mere fancies.

Accept others as they are, and you'll attract supportive friends wherever you go.

The way you *end* a sentence or a paragraph is important. When reading aloud, don't lower your voice on approaching the end of a thought. When writing, don't end a sentence weakly: end on a note of power. When lecturing, end with a downbeat! End with a "punch line." In classical drama, the climax at the end of a play was followed by a brief anticlimax. Good! The anticlimax gave audiences time to relax and absorb what they had experienced. Building toward that climax, however, required a gradual increase of tension, not an increase of anticlimaxes.

Say what you mean, and then stop. People often drag out a thought quite unnecessarily. In writing, in conversation, and very much so in public speaking it is important to be clear, succinct, and *satisfied* with sufficiency!

Remember this always: Your potential for perfection is absolute! To call someone evil is to traduce what he truly is. For all of us, in our souls, are divine. Flotsam seen floating down a river soon drifts out of sight. Similarly, all things move— whether slowly or quickly—toward ultimate bliss. Compare the evil in us to that flotsam. In striving to reach any worthwhile goal, never say, "I have failed." Say, rather, "I haven't yet succeeded!" With that attitude, you *cannot but* succeed in the end.

Look people straight in the eyes—not daringly, as liars do who look *at*, but not *into*, people's eyes—but rather with the wish to *include* other people in your thoughts and feelings.

Speak the truth always, and Nature will support your every undertaking.

Present the truth interestingly. Many people think that being truthful means to be blandly "matter of fact." Bliss, however, is never dull, and is the reality underlying Cosmic Creation itself. In this respect, truth and fact are often very different! Align the truths you speak with the bliss of your own Being.

Honor your commitments, even those you make to yourself. If you've told someone, "I'll buy a newspaper today," and then the news you wanted reaches you by some other means, go buy the paper anyway. Do so to honor your word—to that person, and also to yourself. If you view even your casual commitments as promises, you will gain such a power of truth that your mere word will have support from the universe.

Keep your spine ever straight: It is the channel through which energy flows up to the brain. If that upward flow is weakened or impeded, your power to meet life's challenges will diminish. Truthfulness demands an attitude of firmness, integrity, and clear vision. These virtues all depend on the upward flow of energy in the spine.

Cling to your ideals, even when weakness pulls you repeatedly into delusion. *You are not your mistakes!*

Bathe your heart's sorrows in the clear, purifying water of devotion. View suffering as a layer of mud around your heart, waiting to be hosed away by intense, devotional love.

Be grateful for life's disappointments! Give them to God, and in the end you will always find that they were the best thing that could have happened to you. Disappointments are life's way of opening up for you new windows of opportunity.

To be true to others means to be loyal to them. Truth and loyalty are virtual synonyms. Therefore did my Guru say, "Loyalty is the first law of God." Indeed, disloyalty is worse than untruthfulness, for weakness of character may force a person to be untruthful, but treachery is motivated by no such compulsion: there is merely egoic attachment to delusion.

"There are no such things as obstacles: there are only opportunities!" This teaching of my Guru's might well be engraved over the exit of every home. Obstacles challenge one to summon up more energy in oneself. Without them, people would become lethargic. Indeed, even the worst karma can be a blessing, in the sense that it prods you toward self-improvement.

JUNE 17

Feel the breeze on your skin, then ask yourself, "Whence comes this breath of air? Whither, when it leaves me, will it go?" Let every breeze heighten your awareness of other places, other times, other realities.

JUNE 18

If people disappoint you, never turn against them. Accept the disappointment as a karmic lesson, and tell God firmly, "No matter how the storms of life rage around me, or how heavily the rains fall, how terribly the earth shakes, or how violently circumstances pummel and punish me, I am Thine, ever Thine! Thou art my only truth and polestar in this world!" For your own sake, if for no one else's, emanate kindness to others from your heart. By anger or bitterness you will hurt most of all yourself.

Moods, griefs, and sorrows of every kind cannot be reasoned away. They have their own reality, and their own magnetic attraction. The only way to cure them is to change your level of awareness. When I was young, I used to drive moods and sorrow away by concentrating—once, I did so very fiercely—at the point between the eyebrows.

Heartbreak can be overcome by offering oneself to God. In our realm of duality, life inflicts countless disappointments on everyone. Perfect bliss awaits you only in God. Accept pain as a corrective to mistaken directions in your life. If you live wholeheartedly for God, pain will keep you on the straight path that leads to Him.

Direct every sorrow upward from your heart to the Christ center between the eyebrows. The more determinedly you raise your consciousness from your heart, the closer you will come to understanding this eternal truth: Grief is a delusion born of egoic separation from the true Self, God.

~ **JUNE 22** ~

Acceptance is the first step toward overcoming heartbreak and disappointment. Suffering always arises from wishing that things were other than they are.

~ **JUNE 23** ~

Make communication with others an exchange of vibrations, not only of ideas.

Live *in*, but not *for*, the present moment. In that way you will affirm your inner reality, beyond time and space!

Be good-humored about the shortcomings of others, and you'll find it easier to handle your own. Remember, faults can seem either overwhelming or trivial, depending only on what your imagination makes of them.

Give others credit, where possible, in the anecdotes you tell. Not only will they appreciate the inclusion, but your generosity will loosen the grip of your ego on yourself. Ego is the hidden cause behind all human suffering.

If you want to enjoy life, take yourself less seriously.

To overcome the temptation to tell tales on others, tell good ones on yourself.

Accept criticism impartially. Remember, What *is* simply *is*; and what is not cannot be spoken into existence. Truth, in all things, is the final arbiter.

To develop concentration, do one thing at a time, and *do it well!*

Encourage good ideas, no matter what their source.

If your cause is just, don't be afraid to disappoint others. See to it only that you never disappoint God.

Be loyal to your principles, but never demand that anyone share them. Respect others' right to seek truth in their own way, and at their own pace.

Independence Day in America: The political and national freedom celebrated this day were meant to give all men a chance to rise to their own highest potential. Though independence has not been applied universally, it has at least been directional. It has taken time for black people and for women to win the right to vote, though that right should have been recognized and bestowed from the beginning. It is time now to declare a new kind of freedom: freedom of conscience! This declaration can be made only by and for the individual. Let no one pressure you into thinking or behaving as *he* thinks you ought to. God has a special song to sing through you. It can be offered to the universe only by yourself.

Make contentment your criterion of prosperity. Wealth is primarily the *consciousness* of abundance. Poverty is the *consciousness* of lack. You can be rich though dressed in a hermit's meager clothes and "housed" under a tree. And you can be poor though residing in a marble mansion, served by bustling servants, surrounded by rich furnishings, and possessing a bank account running to many millions. Another criterion of true wealth is indifference to mere opinion. You can know how rich you really are by your measure of inner happiness. If you are burdened with excessive luxury, or imprisoned by the expectations of others, you will pass your life miserably indeed.

My "bottom line" for many years has been not money, profit, or outer success of any kind, but inner peace. I've refused to allow myself to become so stressed as to sacrifice that true wealth. I've even deemed it better—and experience has borne me out—to leave important things undone if my peace might be undermined by giving them attention. For without it, I would be prone to err. From inner peace have come *enlightened* decisions. People's expectations of me can never equal what God Himself expects: my peace in the thought of Him.

Make everyone feel that he or she is special in your eyes—not necessarily special in any particular way, but special above all because everyone on earth is your brother or sister in God.

If someone accuses you of something you once did, say to him, "What matters is not what I did in the past, but what I am today." If you have changed, say so. But if the accusation has no merit, the question of change doesn't arise. If your accuser is right, and you still haven't changed as much as you'd like, reply instead, "Is anyone perfect? And do you think I need your permission to wash my own laundry?" To finish that thought, you might say also, "I am what I am before my conscience and God." In this way, you won't lower yourself to self-justification or counter-accusation. If, on the other hand, your accuser has been vicious, you might reply: "Do your own laundry!"

Encourage others, if you would feel God's encouragement in your heart.

Depend on nothing outside yourself. Find freedom inwardly, by letting no outer circumstance condition your happiness. If a desire arises in your heart, and suggests that something outside yourself will bring you happiness, offer the desire to God. For it is utterly certain—this knowledge is derived from mankind's experience throughout all known history—that in Him alone lies true happiness.

Judge a person (if you must) not by his foibles, but by how sincere he is in his search for truth and for God. The less you judge others, the easier it will be for you to accept yourself as you are. Self-acceptance is the first step, moreover, to self-correction. Remember my Guru's words: "God doesn't mind your faults: He minds your indifference."

Most of the pains we experience, whether physically or mentally, are distressing only if we so define them. Think of them as events, merely, of only slight concern to you. Remove yourself mentally from all outer experiences, and you'll be able to bear pain and suffering with relative ease.

Let no one pressure you with his opinions. Be guided from within yourself. My own family did their best to make me forsake my spiritual calling. I am glad to say I adamantly rejected their pleas. I had my own star to follow. It has led me into the inner temple of peace. Following their wishes would have brought me lasting sorrow, frustration, and disappointment. Therefore I say, *Follow your own star!*

Let no one agitate you. You will never know happiness if you lose your inner peace. If ever you do become distressed, try to calm your heart's feelings by stilling your reactions there. Allow no one to impose on you his hopes, desires, and expectations of you. Even should you find yourself behind prison bars, let no one imprison your mind. Personal integrity is the first and absolute necessity for soul-liberation.

To overcome a judgmental attitude in yourself, observe others whose natures are similarly critical. Are they not merely projecting an inner insecurity? In judging others you only judge yourself. Offer kind acceptance to everyone. In doing so, you will not only deepen your faith in God, but will acquire faith in your own highest potentials.

Isn't it interesting, how people tend to shout on meeting after a long separation! Why all that noise? We might compare those meetings to driving a motorcycle. First there is a high sound, as the motorcycle "revs up." Next comes the low, steady hum, as the desired speed is reached. And notice, finally, the low growl the motor makes as it is turned off. The process might be compared to the three phases of AUM, the Cosmic Vibration: Brahma, the Creator (a relatively high sound); Vishnu, the Preserver (a medium sound); and Shiva, the Destroyer (a low, all-dissolving rumble). Contrasted to people's first meetings, their partings often end on a low note—sometimes of regret; sometimes, if the meeting lacked energy, of dismissiveness. To keep a reunion with friends fresh and interesting, focus especially on the medium—the Vishnu—aspect: Give even more to your reunion than you receive from it. "Fuel" your conversation with inner happiness.

Is there any subject on which you feel sensitive? If so, determine to change yourself. A sore spot on the body tells you there is something wrong there. When people "rub you the wrong way," see what there is in yourself that made you flinch.

When an elder or a superior takes you to task, listen impersonally, but never tell yourself, "Considering the position this person holds, he *must* be right!" People are simply human beings; each has his own faults and weaknesses, which stick to him like burrs until he achieves enlightenment. Indeed, spiritual development, like the sunlight shining through a stained-glass window, may actually *highlight* a person's flaws—until further progress eliminates his ego altogether.

The first and last words of a sentence are espe-cially important. See that your sentences begin and end well. The rest, then, will to a great extent take care of itself.

When traveling anywhere as a tourist, don't be sat-isfied with merely "seeing the sights." Try to feel the vibrations of the places you visit. You will find, in time, that you can actually sense some of their history, and the consciousness of those who lived there long ago. A Mexican friend of mine from the state of Yucatán once related to me a very clear vision he'd had of an ancient temple complex, where Mayans of long ago passed in and out as though they still lived there. Everything you see around you is composed of consciousness. And consciousness emits vibrations, which in turn endure for centuries—perhaps even forever.

Be expansive in your sympathies. Don't limit them to thoughts of "I" and "mine." All men are God's children; so too are you. Be a stranger to no one. The joys and sorrows of all men are your own.

Self-knowledge gives a deep understanding of others. Though some people believe what they want is money, fame, power, pleasure, or material success, their motivation, essentially, is always the same: the longing for bliss. This subtle truth links all beings together in one cosmic family. The deeper you go in this understanding, the more completely you will develop insight into others. You can then even, if you so desire, develop their skills by attuning yourself to their special approach to bliss.

How can one love everyone on earth? Here is one way: Reflect that God's nature is, as the Indian scriptures declare, *Satchidananda*—ever-existing, ever-conscious, ever-new Bliss. He, the Creator, gives to each of us the motivation to seek bliss as our true nature, also. The hidden intention behind every act is the soul's need to discover the secret of existence as perfect bliss. The worst criminal seeks to solve that mystery. He seeks it mistakenly, of course; yet he does so unmistakably. Everyone on earth hungers for that fulfillment, though people usually seek it indirectly. Isn't this reason enough to love, and to be compassionate toward, every being on earth?

Never seek self-justification. If people are interested in hearing your explanation, state the facts simply and impersonally, but never descend (unworthily) to self-defense.

Regardless how people treat you, determine your response to them by the criterion of inner freedom. How others behave is their business. How *you* respond to them is yours. If someone tells you he hates you, will it make you happier to hate him in return? It will be more in your interest to offer him, instead, your sincere friendship.

To be truly creative, work with an attitude of bliss. God's motive in creating the universe was not only, as the Indian scriptures declare, "to enjoy Himself through many." It is also His very bliss-nature to be self-expansive. Despite the widespread suffering on earth, the end of every soul's long, winding, sometimes harrowing journey is perfect bliss—a bliss, as Yogananda put it, "beyond imagination of expectancy."

Meet anger, when possible, with silence, respect, and good will. Don't let anyone's anger shake you from that inner resolve. Peace is the way to avoid all emotional whirlpools. Only by first being inwardly peaceful can your influence for good spread, and bring peace to all.

Why is there so much violence in the world? Surely it is because people are not satisfied with *themselves*! Today's terrorists imagine a world remade in their own image. Should they ever succeed, however, in killing off every-one who falls short of that image, they'd only end up butchering one another! Ultimately, the only way to establish peace on earth is for people everywhere to be peaceful first in themselves.

When others project disharmony toward you, send them in return, from your heart, rays of kindness and harmony. The more consciously you send those thoughts out in blessing, the more others will change. In time they, too, will project only harmony.

To inject uplifting vibrations into whatever you write, try to perfect the word-sequences. These will "work" best if they follow the natural flow of thought. Read each sentence over and over carefully, to ensure the achievement of this flow. Reposition words, phrases, and clauses as necessary for increasing clarity. For instance, in an earlier version of a sentence for July 25 in this book I wrote, "Isn't it in your interest to offer him your sincere friendship in return?" I changed it to read:

"It will be more in your interest to offer him, instead, your sincere friendship." This change places the most important words, "sincere friendship," at the end, making those words linger on in memory. When you do this work for your readers, they will benefit more greatly from what you have to offer them.

In writing, try as much as possible to avoid repeating too closely even such essential words as *and*, *of*, *the*, and *a*. Interchange these last two from time to time. Try to avoid too close a juxtaposition of words that end similarly—for example, words ending in "-ly," "-ity," or "-tion." If you do repeat similar sounds, do so deliberately, for effect. Remember, of course, that every rule can be broken sometimes, depending on the kind of interest you want to awaken. Even speed readers, however, will prefer a flow that is enhanced by right word-sequences.

To know God, it is said that one must possess "the simplicity of a child." How, one wonders—considering the vastness and complexity of the universe—can simplicity be a part of any equation involving true wisdom? The metaphor itself supplies the answer. A child is simple because, although it observes, it doesn't prejudge. Thus, it lives in the present—far more so than most adults whose tendency is to dwell on thoughts of the past or the future. For such adults, the present is hardly more than a connecting bridge. Be childlike in the sense of living *in*, but not *for*, the present. Be childlike, but not childish—not overreacting, that is to say, to pains or slights.

Intuition is simple because it involves direct perception, and is not a process of joining thoughts and ideas together painstakingly like pieces in a jigsaw puzzle. People usually become increasingly complex with the acquisition of knowledge. Learn, instead, to approach your problems not by puzzling them through, but by withdrawing to your own center. There, offer your problems up to that pivotal simplicity. Never feel that you have your answer until you've reached, in your heart, a sense of its perfect rightness.

Invite the participation of others, when possible, in the decisions you make. The more you involve them, the more they will take an interest in, and commit themselves to, working with and helping you.

God's consciousness is center everywhere, circumference nowhere. In that fact lies the secret of divine simplicity. We can most nearly approach such simplicity by imagining God as a *Person* who has nothing to defend, and nothing to promote; who accepts everything as it is; who rejects nothing; who wants nothing from anyone; who sees everything in relation to its eternal, changeless reality; who is wholly without self-importance; who never condescends; and who waits patiently for us, His creatures, to untangle our psychological kinks and recognize that we belong to Him alone. Such is the nature of Absolute Bliss.

God's nature is childlike in this sense: He loves us without being in any way conditioned by our feelings toward Him. He wants nothing from us. His unceasing hope is to welcome us into His infinite home. He is without the slightest ulterior motive. He wants nothing from us but *our* love, and, being complete in Himself, He knows He also has our love, though it be misdirected toward an infinity of worldly desires. He knows it, because what all of us seek is His bliss.

Never reduce people mentally to stereotypes. Everyone is, in his own way, unique. To typecast a person is to impose limitations on him that may paralyze his progress.

Affirm always, as my Guru taught: "What comes of itself, let it come." After every disaster, no matter how great, life goes on—if not in this world, then in some other. An attitude of relaxed acceptance toward whatever happens to you will bring you great inner peace and happiness.

Relax *upward*, toward the spiritual eye in the forehead. Don't try to *force* your concentration to that point. Think of it, rather, as your natural center of being.

Enlist support for your suggestions, but weigh any disagreement carefully, and listen open-mindedly to counter-suggestions.

Notice how quickly the human voice reflects the feelings behind it. An angry person's voice is tight and rigid. Avaricious people tend to speak harshly, almost in a croak. The voice of someone who is arrogant or contemptuous assumes a slightly nasal quality. The voice of one in whom self-interest predominates develops a certain thickness. If one is indifferent to others, his voice will sound flat and dismissive. These tones and many others show the extent to which the voice is both a sounding board for the speaker's state of consciousness, and an affirmation of that state. Listen especially for the warm tone of voice in those who love God. Project outward, through your own voice, a note of kindness, good humor, and generosity. Project above all your devotion to God. The more you focus on letting these qualities vibrate through your voice, the more they will deepen in yourself.

What is the best handshake? People sometimes lightly extend two or three fingers, as if preferring not to touch you at all. Others offer their hand limply, as if eager to disengage from you as quickly as possible. Others cling to your hand as if to a lifeline. Still others squeeze your hand forcefully, as if wanting to overpower you. The best handshake is firm, friendly, and tactfully brief—neither too personal nor too impersonal, and leaving both persons the integrity of their own space.

In inviting others to participate in decisions that are yours to make, the responsibility for the outcome will be yours also. Allow no one's suggestions to become your excuse for failure. Accept only ideas that resonate with your intuition. Never feel obligated to accept a suggestion merely because you have asked for it.

Imagine the worst thing that could happen to you. Then, still imagining, relax your heart and accept it. If you can bear that visualization, inner freedom will be yours. Why not, then, accept whatever comes? Do you fear death? It can't be avoided, so why fear it? When it comes, accept it willingly—even gladly! For know this: You, yourself, can never die.

Whenever possible, give credit to others even if an idea was first your own. Those who keep trying to draw praise to themselves soon find themselves forced also to carry the whole burden of responsibility. To succeed at anything, especially anything *worthwhile*, you will almost always need the help of others. If possible, therefore, involve them even now.

When conversing with people, look at a point in their foreheads between the eyebrows, rather than staring too directly into their eyes. To gaze too fixedly in their eyes may seem an intrusion. If, on the other hand, you look at the floor or at the ground, people may think you resent them. And if you look off to the side, they may think you can't wait to get away from them. If you look up at the ceiling or at the sky, they may suppose you are pondering a point, but if you ponder it too long it will seem to them that, for you, they have ceased to exist. If, then, you gaze at them in the spiritual eye, you may help also to uplift their consciousness.

Speech is naturally melodic. See to it that the melody of your speech be pleasant and attractive. Notice the melodic change that accompanies every shift of mood or feeling. Watch for such changes also in other people. Learn to detect in people's voices their sincerity or insincerity; their aggressiveness, defensiveness, or deceit; their intolerance, kindness, or loyalty. Perception of these qualities depends more on self-knowledge than on specific outer guidelines. Some people can tell a lie so convincingly that even the discriminating may at first be fooled. There are also melodic patterns induced by environment and upbringing; take such cadences into account, to see whether the melody of a person's speech is conditioned or spontaneous.

Accents are important indicators of attitude,
for they derive from more than upbringing and environment. Ego has its center in the medulla oblongata at the base of the brain. Tension at that point tends to draw the head backward, causing one to "look down his nose at the world," and thus to speak with a slightly nasal accent. Aggressive will power makes one force his words out. He therefore emphasizes his consonants. Expression of the kinder emotions tends to soften the consonants and emphasize the vowels. Sounds like *ü* and *ö*, though common in certain languages, also suggest, in the tightening of the lips, an attitude of mild reluctance. Consonants in which the *h* is pronounced in conjunction with *b*, *p*, *t*, and *k* (like the Bengali *bhalo* [good]) are pronounced similarly in all languages when the feelings are expressed emphatically. The American flat *a* is a soft, double sound as in "man" ("ma-uhn," wherein the second sound

is almost inaudible); it sounds sweeter than the same word spoken with an open English accent. The r in the word, "better," sounds warmer and more welcoming in American than in the British English "bettah." On the other hand, the American double "t" sounds muddier and less precise than the English: American, "bedder"; English, "bettah."

Humility is not self-deprecation; it is the simple recognition that, in everything, God alone is the true Doer. God acts through instruments. Humility, though an important step toward overcoming the sense of "I" and "mine," retains some sense of ego—an ego open to higher wisdom and guidance. In total egolessness, even humility ceases to exist; the little self is no longer a consideration.

When giving a gift, think not only whether it is something your friend would enjoy receiving: think also whether *you* would enjoy giving it to him. Gifts should carry vibrations of love and happiness. To give someone a painting that he likes, but that you yourself abominate, would deprive the giving of its essential ingredient: joy.

An excellent way to rise above physical pain is to divert your mind to something else. I've found, for example, when sitting in a dentist's chair (I haven't taken Novocain in years), that mentally composing music, or working out some passage in a book I was writing, helped greatly. The dentist's activities then became hardly noticeable (though often I've heard afterward that the dentist himself was perspiring with sympathetic pain!).

If ever it becomes your duty in life to form a committee, see to it that each member has his own area of responsibility. Much time will be saved if those persons are excluded who, with nothing specific to do, would otherwise talk endlessly to little purpose just to show their involvement in what is going on. Chat sessions are of course different, but when there is work to be done, each committee member should have an area for which he is personally responsible. Thus, when a decision is reached, it can be given to him to implement directly.

Whenever you feel pain or sorrow, withdraw from that feeling to your center in the spine. From there, watch those emotions dispassionately. Tell yourself, "Whatever affects my body and ego can never affect *me*, in my Self. Pain and sorrow—both—are nothing but dreams."

Pretend to yourself that this day is the beginning of a new incarnation. Obviously you aren't a newborn babe, but try to wipe out any power the past has to keep you always doing the same things, making the same mistakes, and performing in the same old ways. Look for new things to accomplish, new worlds to conquer, new ideas to express. Don't be the kind of person who declares pompously, "Well, as I always say . . .": don't be a "psychological antique." Try to be ever-new in yourself and in your relations with friends, loved ones, and even complete strangers.

Today, tell yourself, "I'm going to see life in a new way! When I look at a tree, I will ask myself, 'What message has it for me, from God?' If the trunk is straight, I'll think, 'That is how I shall keep my spine: firmly upright.' If the tree is many-branched, I'll ask myself, 'In what new directions of thought and action can I branch out today?' If the leaves are luxurious, I'll think, 'Let my own life flourish similarly!' And if the tree is bare, let me think (negatively perhaps, at first) 'I don't want my life to be barren!' but then positively: 'I, too, must withdraw sometimes from outer involvement, to return with renewed vigor in confronting life's challenges.'" Everything around you can teach and inspire you, if you animate your gaze with a questing mind.

✑ AUGUST 25 ✑

One way to handle pain and sorrow is to visualize your consciousness expanding in all directions. If, for instance, you are in a dentist's chair, say to yourself, "What happens to this body can touch only a tiny point in the vast reality of my true Self."

Another way to handle pain and sorrow is to tell yourself, "What is happening now is only flotsam on the river of time." What you feel now won't last. Dwell on the thought of eternal bliss, which will be yours once you attain inner freedom.

Live as much as possible at the midpoint between all opposites: That is where the Infinite Spirit dwells. Everything in Creation is dual. Thus did the One become many. Every "up" is canceled by a "down"; light is balanced by darkness; pleasure, by pain; emotional love, by hatred (I say "emotional love," because there is no opposite to divine love, and no balancing opposite to divine joy). Eternal truths lie at the point midway between all opposites. Therefore I say, live more at your center, in the heart.

Offer up all suffering to God. People speak of Christ's suffering on the cross. They don't realize that, in his absolute conquest over ego, he was *happy* to offer his life as a sacrifice for others. He thereby took onto himself their karma. He himself, however, was immune to pain of all kinds. The suffering he felt was for man's indifference to God.

Seek approval only from people whose opinions you respect. The applause of multitudes is like bubbles in a champagne glass, rising, then bursting at the surface. Better the scolding of the wise than the adulation of fools. Popularity is the surest sign of individual inadequacy.

Face every trial cheerfully. Don't shrink from it, but thrust your chest out and accept the test bravely. Remember, you cannot avoid trouble anyway. Trials are like dogs: If they threaten you, confront them with courage and they'll run away! But if you yourself run away, they'll give eager chase.

No calamity will shake you if you can stand calmly and firmly at your own center. "Be able," as my Guru said, "to stand unshaken amid the crash of breaking worlds!" If you offer your heart's feelings up in devotion to God, fear will pass overhead like a cloud, and you will be enveloped in bliss.

Give credit to others for anything you and they have accomplished together. Indeed, give more credit to them than you claim for yourself. I remember my father commenting wryly on the foreword written to a book by the writer's subordinate: "I recommend this book, which was written at my direction and under my constant supervision." What had that old fogey gained, except a few chuckles of derision? If a team helps you, presumably it is because you've needed their help. And if you did need it, thank them by giving them even more credit, perhaps, than they deserve.

Whatever you seek to accomplish, approach it with enthusiasm. Once you've finished it, however, release it into the infinite. If you keep dwelling on past accomplishments, you won't be able to concentrate freely on new ones. I myself find it difficult, sometimes, to remember the names of songs I have written, though I love them all. They're done now, and belong in the past. I have new, fresh images to carve, paint, or otherwise convey.

Think of the setbacks, failures, and disappointments you've had in life. Toss them mentally into the air like flower petals, and watch them float away on the wind, diminishing in size until they disappear altogether. Affirm then, joyously, "In my heart, I am forever free!"

Look at, or imagine, a river flowing constantly. Then visualize your thoughts flowing similarly—not rippling restlessly; not drifting sluggishly; not frozen in fixed opinions like an ice sheet in wintertime. Adapt yourself to circumstances. The more centered you are in your Self, the easier you will find it to change as the needs arise. Affirm silently: "I adapt like flowing water to new situations and ideas."

Devote less time than heretofore to being entertained—by watching television, for instance, or by listening to recorded music. Commit yourself to doing things *yourself*. Don't work from ego, but offer yourself as a clear channel for the Divine Creator. Passivity is to creativity what floating on water is to swimming. And channeling God's grace is to egoic creativity what swimming with the current is to struggling against it.

Be thoughtful when communicating with others. Absent-mindedness induces vagueness, which produces chronic failure. Mean what you say, and say it with focused attention. Thus, you will develop the power to succeed at everything you attempt.

Speak from a center of inner silence. Mere chatter is anesthetizing. A man in Calcutta once asked a younger man, "My boy, are you married?" "What do you mean, Am I married? I'm married to your own daughter!" "Oh, I know, I know. I just wanted to talk, and couldn't think of anything else to say." Wouldn't the older man have done better to remain silent? When you speak from the heart of silence, everything you say will have meaning.

SEPTEMBER 8

Be always, as my Guru put it, "even-minded and cheerful." Watch a cork bobbing ceaselessly about on the surface of a lake: up and down, up and down, never straying in any particular direction, always keeping to one place. Don't be like that cork, bouncing with the ripples of emotion. You'll never get anywhere if you constantly react to what happens around you. Don't imitate: *initiate!* Move serenely through life, like a great ocean liner, centered in the Self within.

SEPTEMBER 9

Be modest—be even self-effacing. But don't belittle yourself. Self-deprecation, too, brings a focus on the ego. There should be neither superiority nor inferiority complex. Concentrate on the *what* of things, not on the *who*.

View your problems dispassionately, as if from a mountain peak. Perspective is lost in the valley of personal involvement. How tiny life's problems are, compared to your spiritual reality! If you allow them to loom large, they may overwhelm you. But if you view them dispassionately, you will see them merely as little specks on the vast panorama of life.

See yourself, when you help others, as a gardener watering his plants. Whether the plants be bushes, grass, or flowers, all of them need water. And human beings, whether haughty or humble, harsh or gentle, ignorant or learned, provocative or submissive, dryly brittle or richly humorous: all of them need nourishment. If you nourish them with the nectar of kindness, they will thrive.

Make a special effort, today, to break out of some self-enclosure—whether of selfishness, or timidity, or personal preoccupation. The growth toward maturity is a matter of escaping from one's ego-prison. Expand your awareness to include the needs of others. Then expand your *feelings*, by sympathizing with those needs. Next, expand your self-identity by helping people to *fulfill* their needs. Finally, release yourself from self-identity altogether by telling yourself, "It is not I who help anyone: I am only a channel for God's grace." The feeling will come to you at last: "He alone is acting through me; He alone is the Doer."

Pay little heed to people's opinions—even to your own! Truth is not a matter of opinion: Truth simply *is*.

Truth cannot be learned: it must be recognized. If you want to guide others to the truth, state your thoughts simply; get people to respect *them* rather than *you* for having stated them. Speak the truth in such a way as to bring it back to people's remembrance. The sage Patanjali defined enlightenment as *smriti*: memory.

In life's race, compete only against yourself. Sooner or later, no matter how skilled you are, there will always be someone better. Every record will be broken; every "best" will be bettered. In the battle between good and evil, seek victory over your ego. Be calmer today than heretofore. Be kinder, more forgiving, more accepting, less judgmental. Whatever your faults or virtues, give increasing energy to that which, in the end, will bring you bliss.

Never complain, no matter what you have to endure. Misfortune lies in your perception of things, not in things themselves. Should you suddenly lose all your wealth—perhaps in a stock market crash—the time may have come in God's plan for you to experience poverty. One positive lesson to be learned from every loss is calm detachment. Another is to become more whole in yourself. Success and failure, equally, are part of life's flow. So too are all the pairs of opposites: wealth and poverty, fame and ignominy, gain and loss of every kind. Accept them with a smile, for only in God can one rise permanently above duality. Meanwhile, whatever your lot in life, accept it with good cheer. Remember, all this is a show—a cosmic dream; a drama. To your deeper Self, life here on earth has no reality.

Concentrate on the details of what you do. At
the same time, refer those details constantly, not
only to your overall purpose, but to a higher end.
Keep the will tuned to life's *true* goal: This is one
of the secrets of genius, which comes from the
superconscious and is inspired by God. Whatever
you do, offer your efforts up to Him for higher
guidance.

SEPTEMBER 18

How shall you define God? Think of Him (or
Her) as the highest potential you can imagine for
yourself. God is all that, and much more. As the
Indian scripture, the Bhagavad Gita, states, He is,
in all things, their supreme manifestation: Perfect
Power, Wisdom, Love, Joy, Peace, Fulfillment,
Satisfaction, Beauty, and Contentment.

When troubles beset you, seek both their cause and their solution in yourself. Karmic law rules supreme everywhere. Your actions of the past represented movement in opposite directions from an unchanging center in yourself. That movement always returns, with equal force, in the opposite direction. Though hindered by what my Guru called "the thwarting crosscurrents of ego," the law must always, sooner or later, be fulfilled. Those myriad back-and-forth movements seldom proceed in a straight line; instead, they create eddies that draw into themselves the debris of countless desires and involvements. Don't upset yourself with life's complexity, but seek the divine simplicity of oneness with God's joy. To do otherwise is to court endless troubles.

You have within yourself the power to over-come all adversity. Even were you to be enslaved, or thrown into a dungeon without hope of release, no one can possess or incarcerate your mind. If you cannot conquer a difficulty out-wardly, rise above it inwardly: Seek freedom in your heart. No one can ever deny you that free-dom. Were utter failure to crash upon you like a giant wave, know that God's law is ever benign and just. Place yourself in His hands, and every-thing must turn out eventually for the best.

If a mood oppresses you, offer it into a wider perception of reality. Moods are like waves: no matter how tall a wave, the ocean level never changes. Live at that point, inwardly, where nothing can affect you.

There is a simple key to happiness: Resolve to *be* happy! Depend not on outer things for what you want in life. Earthly happiness is like a rainbow: radiant with bright colors, but evanescent, for it consists only of raindrops—which, in human life, are the droplets of earthly sorrow! When you learn to welcome the rain as gladly as you smile at a rainbow—the one bringing cleansing to the heart; the other reminding you of God's inner joy—you will be happy always.

True politeness is not a mask. It is a reflection of the innate dignity of the soul. It enables a person to see in everybody, everywhere, the presence of God. Respect all men as your brothers and sisters in the great family of our one common Father/Mother.

View challenges as stimulants to your spiritual ascent. Twice when I was a child, bullies much larger and stronger than I attacked and beat me. Both times I won against them by refusing to admit defeat. Afterward, they avoided me. Never surrender your will to anyone. If you can maintain your integrity, others may accuse you of betrayal, but it is to yourself you must remain true. Let people say about you what they will: Be strong in yourself. If you can preserve your will unbroken, you will always, in the end, come out victorious.

If people treat you condescendingly, don't react. Be polite toward them, but reserved. Let them see that, whatever their opinion of you, they have your respect and good will, but not your deference. Never court anyone's good opinion. Defer to wisdom, but pay no attention to ignorance.

The desire for equality with others is a delusion; we are equal only in the fact that we are all children of God. Life, otherwise, is like a ladder. The lower animals are helped upward in their evolution by association with human beings. Relatively unaware people are helped upward by serving those who are more highly evolved. The caste system in India originally recognized these realities: It wasn't hereditary, and was never intended to be suppressive. It simply indicated the right direction for humanity to develop—from body-bound (*kayastha*) to freedom from ego-bondage. "One moment in the company of a saint," it has been said, "will be your raft over the ocean of delusion." The company of persons more highly evolved than oneself can be uplifting. In the case of the devotee who seeks God, saints are the best company. And best of all is it to be guided by a true guru.

Don't be a social or any other sort of climber, out-wardly. I have observed that game played even in the ashrams of saints. Absorb whatever virtues attract you in others, but never try to impress anybody. Move through life like a large ocean liner: serenely passing through heavy seas. Be whole in yourself. If you see some quality in others that attracts you, invite it aboard as a passenger. Divine illumination will finally carry you beyond all human qualities. Seek only those traits which will assist you in your quest for inner freedom.

What makes a man noble is not land, money, or social position, but character. Be true to your word, generous in giving, kind when faced by any wrong, and courteous to all (even to the lowliest beggar). Always defer to the truth. A truly noble man is one whose character is ever firmly upright.

Good manners are innate. They are born of respect, dignity, and kindness. Customs vary from country to country and from place to place. For those who travel widely, it is impossible to keep abreast of every convention one encounters. Much more important than trivia like table manners are attitudes that ennoble the spirit.

Learn to cooperate with others, even if their interests are different from your own. Never surrender a principle, however, no matter what the consequences to yourself. Your guiding light all your life should be, not egoic self-interest, but God's will. Were you even to be burned at the stake for your loyalty to the truth as you understand it, remember this: Truth alone, in the end, will free you forever from all suffering.

"Fame and wealth," my Guru used to say, "are like prostitutes: loyal to no man." In the end, those two goals, though all but universal, bring only disappointment. If fame comes unsought, owing to some past karma (I hesitate to call that karma *good*!), use it for the benefit of others, rather than to bolster your own pride. Fame can be a means of reaching many people and of helping them, but never glory in it. Whether well known or unknown, you are the same person. It is easier to be yourself, however, if you are unburdened by anyone's expectations of you. Be natural to all: open to their interests, and respectful of their opinions.

Wealth, if it comes to you, should be treated as a sacred trust. It is not really yours, even if you have worked hard to acquire it. Karma (again, it will be *good* karma only if you use it rightly) has given you riches as a means of helping other people. Use your wealth to make this a better world. Otherwise, riches will only suffocate your finer feelings. If they make you feel superior to others, they are a delusion. Treat all human beings as your equals. Remember, a person may be poor financially, but rich in ways that preclude the possession of money. *Appreciate* others for what they are.

Wrap yourself in a cloak of calmness. A calm, wisely guided will is the best protection against adversity.

OCTOBER 4

If you are poor, remember, your karma can be improved. Poverty means that the normal flow of divine abundance has been blocked, in your case, by certain past actions—perhaps of avarice, or selfishness, or indifference to the needs of others, or by scattering your forces heedlessly. You can remove that block by offering your energy into the divine flow. Of course, bad karmic consequences cannot be easily nullified, but their effects *can* be mitigated. The more you allow God to flow through you, the more your every circumstance in life will improve.

OCTOBER 5

If you emanate peaceful thoughts, they'll surround you with a protective aura, and create a barrier against all negativity. Any agitation around you, then, will no longer be able to touch you.

Non-attachment is the true wealth. One who identifies himself with things is always afraid of losing them. And if he fears the loss, he has, in a sense, lost it—at least in his own mind—already. Attachment is an attitude which many people carry to their graves. An old man on his deathbed once cried out to his son, "Trim that lamp wick, son! The oil is running low!" His own life was "running low," and still he worried about saving money! The person of non-attachment wants nothing. And nothing is all anyone really needs, if he is rich in God.

Love all men—if not for themselves (many human traits, after all, are in themselves not lovable!), then for the pure joy of giving love. Everyone is seeking, whether blindly or with clear sight, final fulfillment in God.

Learn when to stop whatever you are doing. If speaking, learn to stop when you've said enough. And if writing, don't drag on beyond your point, once you've made it. People often think, "If I can say just a little more, I'll succeed better in convincing them." After leading your listeners to the top of a cliff, what more can you do except push them over the edge?

Don't worry about others' opinions; don't be concerned with what anyone says or thinks about you—unless you think you might learn something by listening. Think in terms of what you give out to others, not of what you receive from them in return.

Not a thought that you think originates with you. Paramhansa Yogananda wrote, in *Autobiography of a Yogi*, "Thoughts are universally and not individually rooted." Your most precious inspirations are not your own! You have merely caught a current of thought that was already flowing through the universe. Thoughts, in turn, are only manifestations of divine consciousness. Therefore Yogananda said also, "I suffer when you have moods, for I see then that Satan has a hold of you." Think, when negativity wells up within you, "Satan is trying to catch me!" To rid yourself of such "possession," chant to God and raise your level of energy in the spine. Soon you will find positive thoughts and feelings fairly pouring into your mind.

Even if you are not attached to anything, meet life with cheerful expectation. Whatever comes, greet it with a smile. A cheerful attitude will magnetically attract to you, in every circumstance, the best possible results.

Rid yourself of all self-definitions. They block your awareness of yourself as the ever-perfect soul. You, as a manifestation of God, are unique. The Lord never makes even two snow-flakes exactly alike. Self-definitions are like heavy luggage: difficult to carry about, and obstructive to free movement. The more completely you renounce your self-constructs, the easier you will find it, by your openness to soul-guidance, to advance toward freedom. Remember always, you are not this little ego: You are infinite!

Never defend your mistakes. People do that only to protect their pride. The more readily you admit an error, the easier it will be to change yourself. Thus will you win release altogether, eventually, from ego-consciousness.

OCTOBER 14

"People are more important than things." This is a basic principle at our Ananda communities, which my Guru founded through me. It is a good principle for your own life, also. By "things" I don't mean objects only, but plans and projects of all kinds. Consideration for other people will also help to ground your ideas, making them more realistic, and ensuring that what you want to accomplish is right. Remember too, "people" refers not only to others, but also to yourself. Your spiritual progress is more important than anything else in your life.

If you feel impelled to defend a principle, never do so under the influence of anger. Defend your beliefs joyously! *Dharmic*—which is to say, righteous—causes should be defended righteously. And joyous non-attachment is the only way to mount that defense.

Never be afraid to give love, even if others respond to you with disdain. True love wants nothing in return for its gift. It holds out to life no begging bowl, but enriches the giver, and ennobles everyone it touches. If you withhold love from others, on the other hand, you yourself, inside, will die a slow death. For feelings are like flowing water: If they are made to stand still, they will stagnate.

Face trials, obstacles, and challenges courageously. You are a child of God; as such, you are the equal of everyone on earth! Your potential for greatness—indeed, for perfection—is infinite. A painting should be judged, not by any mistakes the artist makes while perfecting his work, but in its finished state.

To be dignified in the true sense does not mean to be proud, pompous, or conceited. *Dignity* is his who lives calmly at his own inner center. A person of true dignity recognizes, and bows to, the divine in all. He keeps his mind open to the views and suggestions of others, but always weighs them first against the understanding he's acquired from his own experience.

Reach out toward others with sympathy: Don't wait for others to reach out first to you. How many wounded there are, stretched out on life's battlefield! Some of them seek to protect themselves from further hurt by a demonstration of cold aloofness. Ignore that attempt: it is merely an act! Become a spiritual medic! Make a special effort to help people who are in psychological pain, or in spiritual doubt. You'll be amazed at what a warm smile can do to melt the blocks of ice that encase so many grieving hearts.

Be humble, but never abject. True humility is not self-abasement: it is the contemplation of, and complete absorption in, a broader reality than one's own. In bright sunlight, a burning candle is so dimmed that it shines unobserved.

Give others their due. Indeed, to make sure your gift is not grudging, give them *more* than their due. In that spirit of generosity, allow others to give you what is your due also. Remind them always, however, that God is the Doer. To *reject* sincere praise in the name of humility would be to impugn the judgment and good taste of the one who offered it.

Never allow yourself, out of hurt feelings, to close your heart's door to anyone. Locking it will only cause you pain. You can no more control how others treat you than you can the weather. How you behave toward them, however, is yours to control. Rather than let any hurt block your heart, ask yourself, "Is there any point in suffering twice?"

If you want to succeed in life, concentrate your powers. No one, if he wishes to penetrate a field of ice, presses down on the whole field. He drills with a sharp instrument at one point. Similarly, the densest obstacle can be penetrated by calm, focused intention. By seeking God through the little opening of your own ego, you will soon find yourself swimming in the sea of cosmic bliss.

Stand by whatever lessons you've learned from life. People may urge you to see things their way, but the only truth you can ever really know is one you've experienced for yourself. Change your mind only when new experience obliges you to see things differently.

If you see anything in others that displeases you, ask yourself, "Does it really matter? There are so many wrongs in this world! The best I can do is simply to give up being displeased!" What we don't like in others is usually a reflection of some fault we have in ourselves. What we dislike in the world, too, usually points to something we need to change in ourselves—at least in terms of willingness to accept the inevitable. Learn to accept life as it is. I don't say, Never try to improve matters. Do improve them if you can, always calmly and in support of the good. But realize that there are simply too many wrongs in the world for all of them to be improved very much. Your first need, always, is to remain calm and undisturbed in your Self.

Dare to dream greatness. Seek it above all, however, in the sight of God, not in human eyes. To seek approval from people is like building a house on a bog. Approval is worthwhile only if it comes from those whose loyalty is first to truth. To dream greatness is not a presumption, if one aspires to do great, noble deeds that will inspire others. Try, above all, to fulfill *God's will* for you. Ask His help in your efforts to help others.

Wish everyone the best, and, whatever specific individuals do, life itself will always support you. Bless everybody, and you will yourself be blessed. We receive back from the world in exact proportion to what we give out to it, and with the same intensity.

Has something or someone angered or upset you? If so, work on correcting that emotion in yourself. Just think: Someday—perhaps even later this very day—you'll find yourself involved in other concerns. Emotions don't last. Why let yourself stew in that pot? It is *you* who are being cooked! Don't react until you've restored your own equilibrium.

Think of yourself as a student of truth, and of life; never as anybody's teacher. If your duty in life is, in fact, to teach others, consider what a privilege it is to share with them what you've learned from life. Never feel that anyone owes it to you to accept what you tell him.

OCTOBER 30

If you are angry, it may be only because your idea of how things ought to have been has been outraged. Reflect on how many views can be held on any subject. Seek the rest point in yourself, midway between the pairs of opposites. Dwell there calmly. In inner stillness you'll be able to address every issue effectively.

OCTOBER 31

If your emotions become upset, drink the antidote to every emotional poison: kindness. Be like Jesus, who calmed a storm by commanding the waves: "Peace. Be still!" Disturbed emotions can affect the whole body: the digestion, the nervous system, the heart rate, the breath, even one's mental clarity. Is it really worth all that trouble over things you probably couldn't change if you tried to?

Never accuse or confront anyone. First ask him, as supportively as possible, "Did you do it?" If he says yes, then ask him, "Why?" Give him the benefit of the doubt. If no doubt exists, respect at least his right to make his own mistakes. Thus, he will know you for a supportive friend. And isn't that a consideration you yourself would like from everyone?

Make everything you do an act of self-giving. Thus you will combat natural egoism, and expand the boundaries of your reality to include the realities of others.

Egotism, and egoism: a friend of mine once asked me the difference, and I replied almost without thinking, "Egotism is pride, whereas egoism is excessive consciousness of oneself." I still consider that the best explanation of the difference. We need to overcome both qualities, but of the two, egoism is the subtler and the more insidious. The best way out of it is to *give* of oneself—to others; to what one believes in; to God.

Keep a sense of humor, especially when things don't turn out as you hoped. Life is a play. Often, indeed, it is a tragicomedy. You will enjoy it best if you can remain unaffected. Even if the play ends in tragedy, it may help to purify your heart, and to expand your consciousness.

Consideration for other people is a sign of maturity; it shows openness to different realities from one's own, and is necessary to man's struggle to pull himself out of the mud of egoism.

Never accept an idea merely because others endorse it. As long as you are true to yourself, and to your understanding of what is right and wrong, it won't matter if, in other people's eyes, you seem quaint or passé. The road to truth can sometimes be quite rough, but it leads toward ever-increasing clarity. The smooth highway of popularity, on the other hand, meanders through dense fogs of delusion into deeper and deeper darkness.

Dress not for admiration, but rather to give others pleasure. Often I have gone out of my way to thank a perfect stranger, male or female, for wearing something colorful and pleasing to the eye. Color especially, if it is well chosen, can make everyone's day a little brighter. When thanking people, however, try never to give the impression that you may have some ulterior motive for doing so.

When others are speaking idly, don't be drawn into that light chatter. Be respectful, but remain somewhat apart—perhaps even silent. Idle chatter, like radio static, disturbs the perception of underlying realities.

One's taste in food can indicate, and can also influence, his state of consciousness. Eat only foods that are rich in life-force and energy. Some foods are stale, and virtually "dead," lacking, as they do, all vitality. For human beings, fresh fruits and vegetables are the best. Don't eat foods that are either excessively stimulating or excessively bland. Foods convey distinct vibrations, which affect one's consciousness. It is therefore good to avoid eating meat, especially the meat of animals that are intelligent enough to know they are being slaughtered, and that therefore experience such violent emotions as fear and anger. Fish, fowl, or lamb are better for those who crave meat. In consuming the flesh of more highly evolved animals, however, such as pigs or cattle, one absorbs harmful emotions into oneself.

In judging good taste in the arts, ask yourself, "What does this (piece of music; this painting; this carving; this poem, drama, or novel) do to my state of mind? Has it a soothing or an uplifting influence? Does it help to induce in myself a state of harmony, or wisdom, or some other high quality?" To produce good art requires far more than skill, for art represents states of consciousness. Ask yourself, "Would I like to receive someone into my home who demonstrates these qualities in his work?"

If you find people unreceptive to your wit, don't bludgeon them with it. Having offered a thought in fun, retain your good spirits. Be kind, but respect others' right to see things their own way.

Make no special effort to be stylish.
People reveal in modishness their own lack of taste. One wonders if the styles displayed in the fashion sections of newspapers and magazines aren't actually *intended* to shock. Their message seems to be only, "Look at me! Look even in horror and dismay. But look!" It is difficult to imagine a stylish person being humble. Good taste seems to go with understatement. Indeed, understatement is the very essence of good taste.

Be graceful in your movements. Awkward or jerky gestures reflect, and also induce, disconnected thinking. But grace of movement will help bring a smooth flow to all your thinking.

Before making an important decision in life, enter into your inner temple of silence, and there consult your higher Self. If your mind is focused, you may get your answer in an instant. Direct your question to God through the spiritual eye in your forehead. The answer will then appear in your heart as a deep, calm intuition. If you are not yet sure, ask, "Is this the right decision? If not, what ought I to do?" The correctness of the answer will depend on how one-pointedly you focus your energy. Some people take months to reach a conclusion they might have reached in a moment, if they'd concentrated deeply. Often they reach wrong conclusions anyway, simply because they expected their answer to be *reasonable*!

Inspire others more by your example than by what you say. Next, seek to inspire them even more by your vibrations than by your example. An act of kindness may not be understood in the spirit you intended, but *vibrations* of kindness will influence people's feelings, changing them from within. Kindness is a vibration of consciousness, and therefore has no boundaries.

Seek guidance less from reason than from inspired feeling. For although suppressed emotions will distort the clarity of your perception, inspired feeling is intuition. In everything you do, tune in to that clarity, and you'll always be guided correctly.

NOVEMBER 17

Have the courage to embrace the unexpected. Life is an ever-new drama. If you meet it with positive expectations, you will turn every challenge to good advantage.

NOVEMBER 18

Give praise sincerely, but understatedly. Never flatter anyone. Praise the God in others, but not their egos, for you, as their friend, ought always to support their aspirations toward the spiritual heights.

NOVEMBER 19

Think before you speak. Be circumspect both in speech and in deed. Don't, by unseemly haste, expose yourself to misunderstandings. Why embroil yourself in unnecessary controversy?

Receive praise good-humoredly. Reflect that whatever compliments you receive today may become brickbats tomorrow! Even deserved praise, if accepted too personally, may only add to one's already-heavy burden of self-definitions. In your quest for happiness, neglect no opportunity to lighten that load.

Don't compare yourself with others to either your advantage or their detriment. On a freeway, as many cars precede you as follow behind. Once you are in front of one cluster, you will only find yourself last in the next one. Resolve simply to go your own way, intent wholly on reaching your own destination.

Your magnetism depends on two things: your strength of will, and your level of awareness. Never impose your will on anyone. Let your influence be like a golden aura of light, surrounding you wherever you go. Project it invitingly to others. Leave it to them to accept as much from you, or as little, as they choose.

Flow through life as though on a downhill ski run. Don't puzzle your way through it as if playing a game of chess, plotting each move carefully in advance. Bring spontaneity to everything you do. The smooth flow of intuition can be disrupted by too-careful reasoning. Rely more on soul-guidance.

Criticize no one, even if the criticism is deserved. For your words may discourage, by suggesting that improvement is impossible. Only persons of strong will power can turn negative judgment of them to good account with a strong, positive affirmation. Many years ago, disciples senior to me in my Guru's work tried (out of envy, I think) to destroy my faith in myself. I prayed, later, "Divine Mother, they are right: I *am* nothing. You alone are my strength and my guide." After all, didn't even an ugly duckling once became a swan? Their scathing condemnation proved one of the greatest blessings of my life; it freed me to serve my Guru in ways that he himself had asked of me. Was their karma good or bad for the way they treated me? I suspect they'll have to pay at least for their *intentions*. For their clear purpose was to destroy me. Ill will, like a ball attached with a rubber band to a paddle, cannot but snap back upon the paddle itself.

Seek wisdom more from experience than from books. When reading advice in a book, ask yourself, "Does this counsel resonate with my own experience?" If not, put it on "hold." Don't scoff at it, for it may contain truths you haven't yet discovered for yourself. But accept nothing on blind faith. Only when a truth has been lived can it be wholly known.

Be loyal above all to truth as you yourself understand it. Always tell the truth, moreover, no matter how inconvenient you find it. Friends and relatives may try to influence you otherwise, but be like a compass needle: Point ever toward the polestar of your own integrity.

Always listen inwardly for the voice of wise counsel. If you keep yourself fully open, you may hear suggestions even in the wind.

Make originality your philosophy of life—not in the sense of trying to be different, but rather of being true to your origin in God. Originality in this sense doesn't mean doing something that has never been done before. It means developing your own perception of the truth. The same thoughts may have occurred already to millions of people, but if the thoughts rise with fresh energy from soul-consciousness, they will never grow stale. How many lovers through the ages have exclaimed, "I love you"! Yet when the words were spoken sincerely, they never palled.

Think of others not as your competitors,
but as your colleagues, even when working in the same field of endeavor as they. A thousand rivulets, conjoining, become a mighty river. Thus, indeed, are great civilizations born.

In recreation, seek to re-create yourself.
During every pause in your activity, seek in inner peace a renewal of your creative spirit. Withdraw into your inner temple of silence, and, there, focus on re-energizing every thought, every feeling.

Expect success, but don't let the expectation replace painstaking effort. People who brag about what they will accomplish, someday, usually overlook the little steppingstones of details that are required, to reach success.

Do your best, then leave the outcome in God's hands. Attachment to results will only diminish your ability to work effectively in the present. Without attachment to results, even failure will free you to redirect your energies anew, and ever yet anew, until success is achieved.

Do nothing for applause. Act for the far-more-satisfying approval of your own conscience. Someone once asked me, "What has motivated you to do all the things you've done in your life?" Conscience? yes, certainly. But conscience in reaction to the sorrows I had seen in the world, brought on by people's ignorance of who and what they really were, as children of our universal Father/Mother God.

Don't ask yourself, "How can I approach my tasks differently?" Don't even ask, "How can I do them better?" until you've asked first, "What is the right thing to do, and the *right* way to go about doing it?"

Show respect for convention, but remember that conventions are often started by unconventional people. Why do people stand when their national anthems are being played? It probably began with one deeply moved individual; nobody wanted to show disrespect, so everyone followed his example. Why do people stand for the "Hallelujah" chorus in Handel's *Messiah*? Because King George of England did so first, and everyone had to do likewise. Most conventions have no intrinsic meaning. Usually it would be making only a foolish statement to rebel against them; they are the lubricant which keeps the machinery of society functioning smoothly. Follow convention, then, to be sociable, but *respect* it only if reason tells you it serves some good purpose. Ignore conventions that demean any particular social group.

Some conventions must be changed, certainly.
Racial discrimination in America is a national disgrace, for it places fetters on the egos of all who practice it. So too is the caste system in India. That system, however, had an enlightened origin before it became hereditary. It pointed the way to liberation for all mankind. When caste became hereditary, the same abomination appeared as with racial discrimination in America. Everyone on earth is your brother or sister in God. Respect all as fellow pilgrims on the path to our final abode of Bliss.

Practice patience: It is the shortest path to success. Patience will keep you calm in the face of difficulties, and will enable you to meet each obstacle effectively.

Let others see you, if they are so inclined, as their enemy. Resolve for your part to be their friend. More than one person in my life has said to me, "I don't know why, but I hate you!" Well, *I* know why: I am true to myself, not to their desires or expectations of me. But I always answer them, "I know only that I am your friend, and will always be your well-wisher."

To attract abundance in your life, see money as a flow of energy, not as a static quantity. See life in the same way: as a flowing river, not as fixed patterns of behavior. Leave your ego on the bank, and enter the stream of cosmic awareness. There are no limits to how much of life's abundance can be yours, if you will plunge into the divine current and swim there joyously.

If you want to improve your circumstances, work first on improving yourself. To desire better treatment from others is, in a sense, to enslave yourself to them. Become a cause in life, not an effect. Self-dependence is independence, and a mark of true heroism.

Attachment binds one to things in the way that unripe fruit clings to its branch, even when buffeted by high winds. Be like a ripe fruit, which instantly drops when it is brushed by a mere breeze. At the slightest hint of adversity, remember God, and release your grasp on the tree-branch of delusion.

Include the success of *others* in your efforts to succeed, yourself. Better a stream that makes green a whole valley than an oasis surrounded by vast stretches of sand.

A true friend is one with whom you can weep, and not only laugh. Be a true friend to all. Let them feel that you care for them. Weep with them not to increase their sorrow, but to wean them from it altogether. Don't weep for yourself, however. To be a best friend to all—to yourself as well— strive always to find a way out of darkness into light.

Love others as extensions of your own Self. See everyone as specializing on behalf of the whole human race in being himself.

If someone ridicules you, laugh *with* him if you can. But if his ridicule is mere buffoonery, quietly look away and say nothing. And if he mocks your principles, answer him as he deserves: "Mockery comes easily, to the ignorant." Has someone slighted you? Thank him. Has someone hurt your feelings? Thank him. Every blow to your ego can boost your soul-awareness. On the other hand, if someone tries to destroy your work, protect it, but be thankful for the reminder that everything is *maya*: delusion. True fulfillment will be yours only when you've escaped Satan's clutches forever.

Think vastness! Think eternity! Don't be limited to your present realities. See your thoughts as waves on the vast ocean of cosmic awareness.

As you wash your body daily, so also, before going to bed in the evening, cleanse your heart of all impure desires and attachments. Free your mind of wrong thoughts, and offer yourself into the clear stream of Divine Bliss.

Imagine every difficulty, every desire, every attachment soaring up and away from you like a balloon, growing smaller with distance until it disappears. Then return to your essential Self, and enjoy your release into infinite freedom.

The Italians have a saying, *"Se non è vero, è ben trovato*: If it isn't true, at least it's well said." Don't, however, be lured too far from your own center by the attractive power of epigrams. Where truth is concerned, laugh if you feel to, but in the end, be serious.

How modern do we owe it to ourselves to be? I myself was born in the then-backward, nearly medieval land of Romania. Never have I made a great effort to bring myself into the modern age. Scientific discoveries have swirled around me. New fads have sprung up. New slang has been tossed merrily from person to person. New ways of looking at things have popped up like jacks-in-the-box. I have chosen to keep myself a little apart from it all, accepting only as much of it as would help me. (These pages, for instance, are being written on a computer.) I say: Pass serenely through life's fairground of excitements, but let nothing touch you that might take you out of yourself. I myself never watch television, unless for some very specific purpose. I don't care to be either modern or old-fashioned. Time passes, but divine truth remains forever the same. Why not live in timelessness?

Work at simplifying your view of life. Seek the simple unity beneath life's endlessly bewildering complexity. Complexity, whether in work or in relationships, only creates more complexity. To be divinely childlike means to discover perfect oneness in God's bliss.

Emanate peace in all directions from your heart. Harmonize the vibrations there; then radiate them out to your environment. Feel them entering all hearts, everywhere.

Give up thinking, "This is mine! all mine!" Tell God, with regard to everything in your life, "This is Thine! all Thine! Nothing is my own except under franchise from Thee." The less you think of anything as your own, the freer in yourself you will be. And the more you think of everything as His, the more joy will thrill your heart, until you yourself become pure Bliss.

Never depend on your own powers alone.

They are inevitably fragile, weak, and inconsistent. But if you place your trust in God, you will find that He readily meets your needs. Ask Him with faith; don't plead or wheedle with Him. Say, rather, "This is what I am trying to accomplish for You. I need Your strength and guidance to do it well. I'll do what I can, but *You* have to do the rest." Don't be afraid that you might offend Him by your presumption. Why should He mind? If your desire is to please Him, how can He not approve? Before beginning many a job that I later completed successfully, I've said to Him, "I can't do this on my own, but *You* can do anything! So come along now: Help me!"

The teachings of Jesus Christ, and of every great spiritual master, are as fresh, true, and alive today as when they were first declared. Truth never changes with time. Its expression may vary with fluctuations in human understanding, but love, wisdom, and joy are eternal realities. There is no need to "pound your pulpit," emotionally. All that anyone needs is the awareness that Truth, as taught in all true scriptures, is forever one. Our souls came from God, and our divine assignment is to merge back at last into Him.

To be creative, first relax your mind, then offer it up to God. Every worthwhile accomplishment was conceived first in the Infinite.

You belong to all nations. Only temporarily are you an American, Frenchman, Italian, Indian; Christian, Jew, Hindu, Buddhist, or Muslim. You belong to all classes. Your social status is only temporarily upper, middle, or lower. No human condition can define you, for you are the pure soul, descended from God who, for all eternity, is your essential, ever-changeless Reality.

Direct energy consciously into everything you do. Remember, energy has its own intelligence, and responds willingly to proper guidance. It can make things happen for you that you yourself could not have even planned.

Never identify anyone with his personality.
Define him, rather, by his intentions, and by the sincerity with which he seeks truth. The personality is only a product of actions and reactions over countless incarnations. The innate goodness of one's intentions, however, has its origins at their furthest depths, in the Self.

Respect excellence wherever you find it. True excellence is often the result of group endeavor, but it requires in every case the personal commitment of energy and awareness. Excellence, like everything else that is worthwhile, springs from *within* the Self.

Develop a sense of community with others. No one in this world stands alone, though in many ways the opposite seems true, since we come into this life alone and must leave it again at death, quite alone. Yet we come into a welcoming family, and should so live our lives that others weep when we leave this world. Everything we do in our solitary-seeming comings and goings depends, to a great extent, on others. Expand your sense of community to include an ever-larger number of people, until you see everyone on earth as belonging to your own family, in God.

About the Author

"Swami Kriyananda is a man of wisdom and compassion in action, truly one of the leading lights in the spiritual world today."
——Lama Surya Das, Dzogchen Center, *author of Awakening The Buddha Within*

Swami Kriyananda

A prolific author, *accomplished composer, playwright, and artist, and a world-renowned spiritual teacher, Swami Kriyananda refers to himself simply as "a humble disciple" of the great God-realized master, Paramhansa Yogananda. He met his guru at the age of twenty-two, and served him during the last four years of the Master's life. And he has done so continuously ever since.*

Kriyananda was born in Romania of American parents, and educated in Europe, England, and the United States. Philosophically and artistically inclined from youth, he soon came to question life's meaning and society's values. During a period of intense inward reflection, he discovered Yogananda's *Autobiography of a Yogi*, and immediately traveled three thousand miles from New York to California to meet the Master, who accepted him as a monastic disciple. Yogananda appointed him as the head of the monastery, authorized him to teach in his name and to give initiation into Kriya Yoga, and entrusted him with the missions of writing, lecturing, and developing what he called "world brotherhood colonies."

Recognized as "the father of the spiritual communities movement" in the United States, Swami Kriyananda founded Ananda World Brotherhood Village in the Sierra Nevada foothills of Northern California in 1968. It has served as a model for seven communities founded subsequently in the United States, Europe, and India.

In 2003 Swami Kriyananda, then in his seventy-eighth year, moved to India with a small international group of disciples to dedicate his remaining years to making his guru's teachings better known in that country. He has established Ananda's third publishing company, all of which publish his one hundred-plus literary works and spread the teachings of Kriya Yoga throughout the world. His vision for the upcoming years includes, in India, founding cooperative spiritual communities (two communities already exist there, one in Gurgaon and the other near Pune); a temple of all religions dedicated to Yogananda; a retreat center; a school system; a monastery; as well as a university-level Yoga Institute of Living Wisdom.

MORE YOGANANDA TITLES

The original 1946 unedited edition of
Yogananda's spiritual masterpiece

AUTOBIOGRAPHY OF A YOGI

by Paramhansa Yogananda

Autobiography of a Yogi is one of the best-selling Eastern philosophy titles of all time, with millions of copies sold, named one of the best and most influential books of the twentieth century. This highly prized reprinting of the original 1946 edition is the only one available free from textual changes made after Yogananda's death. Yogananda was the first yoga master of India whose mission was to live and teach in the West.

In this updated edition are bonus materials, including a last chapter that Yogananda wrote in 1951, without posthumous changes. This new edition also includes the eulogy that Yogananda wrote for Gandhi, and a new foreword and afterword by Swami Kriyananda, one of Yogananda's close, direct disciples.

This edition of *Autobiography of a Yogi* is also available in unabridged audiobook (MP3) format, read by Swami Kriyananda, Yogananda's direct disciple.

Praise for Autobiography of a Yogi

"In the original edition, published during Yogananda's life, one is more in contact with Yogananda himself. While Yogananda founded centers and organizations, his concern was more with guiding individuals to direct communion with Divinity rather than with promoting any one church as opposed to another. This spirit is easier to grasp in the original edition of this great spiritual and yogic classic."

— David Frawley, Director, American Institute of Vedic Studies,
author of *Yoga and Ayurveda*

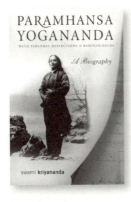

PARAMHANSA YOGANANDA

A Biography with Personal Reflections and Reminiscences

by Swami Kriyananda

Paramhansa Yogananda's classic *Autobiography of a Yogi* is more about the saints Yogananda met than about himself—in spite of the fact that Yogananda was much greater than many he described. Now, one of Yogananda's few remaining direct disciples relates the untold story of this great spiritual master and world teacher: his teenage miracles, his challenges in coming to America, his national lecture campaigns, his struggles to fulfill his world-changing mission amid incomprehension and painful betrayals, and his ultimate triumphant achievement. Kriyananda's subtle grasp of his guru's inner nature reveals Yogananda's many-sided greatness. Includes many never-before-published anecdotes.

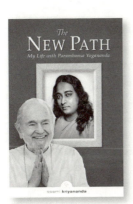

THE NEW PATH

My Life with Paramhansa Yogananda

by Swami Kriyananda

This is the moving story of Kriyananda's years with Paramhansa Yogananda, India's emissary to the West and the first yoga master to spend the greater part of his life in America. When Swami Kriyananda discovered *Autobiography of a Yogi* in 1948, he was totally new to Eastern teachings. This is a great advantage to the Western reader, since Kriyananda walks us along the yogic path as he discovers it from the moment of his initiation as a disciple of Yogananda. With winning honesty, humor, and deep insight, he shares his journey on the spiritual path through personal stories and experiences. Through more than four hundred stories of life with Yogananda, we tune in more deeply to this great master and to the teachings he brought to the West. This book is an ideal complement to *Autobiography of a Yogi*.

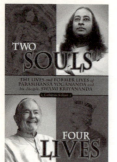

TWO SOULS: FOUR LIVES

The Lives and Former Lives of Paramhansa
Yogananda and his disciple, Swami Kriyananda
Catherine Kairavi

This book explores an astonishing statement
made by Paramhansa Yogananda, that he was
the historical figure, William the Conqueror, in a
previous incarnation.

The Norman Conquest of England was one of the
pivotal moments in world history, a series of events that affects us even
today. Is it possible that two of the greatest men of that era—William the
Conqueror and his son, Henry I of England—have recently reincarnated
as the great spiritual master Paramhansa Yogananda (author of the classic
Autobiography of a Yogi) and his close disciple, Swami Kriyananda? If so,
what are the subtle connections between the Norman Conquest and
modern times?

THE ESSENCE OF THE BHAGAVAD GITA

Explained by Paramhansa Yogananda
As Remembered by his disciple, Swami Kriyananda

Rarely in a lifetime does a new spiritual classic
appear that has the power to change people's lives
and transform future generations. This is such a
book. This revelation of India's best-loved scripture
approaches it from a fresh perspective, showing
its deep allegorical meaning and its down-to-earth
practicality. The themes presented are universal:
how to achieve victory in life in union with the divine; how to prepare for
life's "final exam," death, and what happens afterward; how to triumph over
all pain and suffering.

"A brilliant text that will greatly enhance the spiritual life of every reader."
—Caroline Myss, author of *Anatomy of the Spirit* and *Sacred Contracts*

*"It is doubtful that there has been a more important spiritual writing in the
last fifty years than this soul-stirring, monumental work. What a gift! What
a treasure!"*
—Neale Donald Walsch, author of *Conversations with God*

REVELATIONS OF CHRIST

Proclaimed by Paramhansa Yogananda
Presented by his disciple, Swami Kriyananda

The rising tide of alternative beliefs proves that now, more than ever, people are yearning for a clear-minded and uplifting understanding of the life and teachings of Jesus Christ. This galvanizing book, presenting the teachings of Christ from the experience and perspective of Paramhansa Yogananda, one of the greatest spiritual masters of the twentieth century, finally offers the fresh perspective on Christ's teachings for which the world has been waiting. *Revelations of Christ* presents us with an opportunity to understand and apply the scriptures in a more reliable way than any other: by studying under those saints who have communed directly, in deep ecstasy, with Christ and God.

"This is a great gift to humanity. It is a spiritual treasure to cherish and to pass on to children for generations."

—Neale Donald Walsch, author of *Conversations with God*

"Kriyananda's revelatory book gives us the enlightened, timeless wisdom of Jesus the Christ in a way that addresses the challenges of twenty-first century living."

—Michael Beckwith, Founder and Spiritual Director, Agape International Spiritual Center, author of *Inspirations of the Heart*

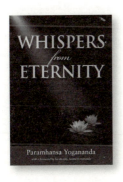

WHISPERS FROM ETERNITY

Paramhansa Yogananda
Edited by his disciple, Swami Kriyananda

Many poetic works can inspire, but few, like this one, have the power to change your life. Yogananda was not only a spiritual master, but a master poet, whose verses revealed the hidden divine presence behind even everyday things. This book has the power to rapidly accelerate your spiritual growth, and provides hundreds of delightful ways for you to begin your own conversation with God.

Swami Kriyananda (J. Donald Walters)

CONVERSATIONS WITH YOGANANDA

Recorded, Compiled, and Edited with commentary by his disciple Swami Kriyananda

This is an unparalleled, first-hand account of the teachings of Paramhansa Yogananda. Featuring nearly 500 never-before-released stories, sayings, and insights, this is an extensive, yet eminently accessible treasure trove of wisdom from one of the 20th Century's most famous yoga masters.

"A wonderful book! To find a previously unknown message from Yogananda now is an extraordinary spiritual gift. Open up at random for an encouraging word from one of the century's most beloved spiritual teachers."

—Neale Donald Walsch, author of *Conversations with God*

THE ESSENCE OF SELF-REALIZATION

The Wisdom of Paramhansa Yogananda
Recorded, Compiled, and Edited
by his disciple Swami Kriyananda

With nearly three hundred sayings rich with spiritual wisdom, this book is the fruit of a labor of love that was recorded, compiled, and edited by his disciple, Swami Kriyananda. A glance at the table of contents will convince the reader of the vast scope of this book. It offers as complete an explanation of life's true purpose, and of the way to achieve that purpose, as may be found anywhere.

The WISDOM of YOGANANDA series

Six volumes of Paramhansa Yogananda's timeless wisdom in an approachable, easy-to-read format. The writings of the Master are presented with minimal editing, to capture his expansive and compassionate wisdom, his sense of fun, and his practical spiritual guidance.

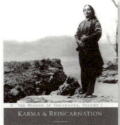
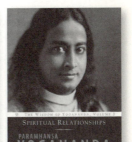

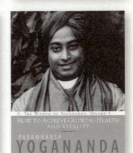

HOW TO BE HAPPY ALL THE TIME
The Wisdom of Yogananda Series, VOLUME 1

Yogananda powerfully explains virtually everything needed to lead a happier, more fulfilling life. Topics include: looking for happiness in the right places; choosing to be happy; tools and techniques for achieving happiness; sharing happiness with others; balancing success and happiness; and many more.

KARMA & REINCARNATION
The Wisdom of Yogananda Series, VOLUME 2

Yogananda reveals the truth behind karma, death, reincarnation, and the afterlife. With clarity and simplicity, he makes the mysterious understandable. Topics include: why we see a world of suffering and inequality; how to handle the challenges in our lives; what happens at death, and after death; and the purpose of reincarnation.

SPIRITUAL RELATIONSHIPS
The Wisdom of Yogananda Series, VOLUME 3

This book contains practical guidance and fresh insight on relationships of all types. Topics include: how to cure bad habits that can end true friendship; how to choose the right partner; sex in marriage and how to conceive a spiritual child; problems that arise in marriage; the Universal Love behind all your relationships.

HOW TO BE A SUCCESS
The Wisdom of Yogananda Series, VOLUME 4

This book includes the complete text of The Attributes of Success, the original booklet later published as The Law of Success. In addition, you will learn how to find your purpose in life, develop habits of success and eradicate habits of failure, develop your will power and magnetism, and thrive in the right job.

HOW TO HAVE COURAGE, CALMNESS, & CONFIDENCE
The Wisdom of Yogananda Series, VOLUME 5

~ Winner of the 2011 International Book Award for Best Self-Help Title ~

This book shows you how to transform your life. Dislodge negative thoughts and depression. Uproot fear and thoughts of failure. Cure nervousness and systematically eliminate worry from your life. Overcome anger, sorrow, over-sensitivity, and a host of other troublesome emotional responses; and much more.

HOW TO ACHIEVE GLOWING HEALTH & VITALITY
The Wisdom of Yogananda Series, volume 6

Paramhansa Yogananda, a foremost spiritual teacher of modern times, offers practical, wide-ranging, and fascinating suggestions on how to have more energy and live a radiantly healthy life. The principles in this book promote physical health and all-round well-being, mental clarity, and ease and inspiration in your spiritual life. Readers will discover the priceless Energization Exercises for rejuvenating the body and mind, the fine art of conscious relaxation, and helpful diet tips for health and beauty.

FURTHER EXPLORATIONS

THE RUBAIYAT OF OMAR KHAYYAM EXPLAINED
Paramhansa Yogananda, edited by Swami Kriyananda

The Rubaiyat is loved by Westerners as a hymn of praise to sensual delights. In the East its quatrains are considered a deep allegory of the soul's romance with God, based solely on the author Omar Khayyam's reputation as a sage and mystic. But for centuries the meaning of this famous poem has remained a mystery. Now Yogananda reveals the secret meaning and the golden spiritual treasures hidden behind the Rubaiyat's verses, and presents a new scripture to the world.

THE BHAGAVAD GITA

According to Paramhansa Yogananda
Edited by Swami Kriyananda

This translation of the Gita, by Paramhansa Yogananda, brings alive the deep spiritual insights and poetic beauty of the famous battlefield dialogue between Krishna and Arjuna. Based on the little-known truth that each character in the Gita represents an aspect of our own being, it expresses with revelatory clarity how to win the struggle within between the forces of our lower and higher natures.

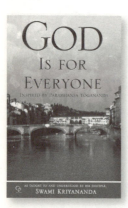

GOD IS FOR EVERYONE

Inspired by Paramhansa Yogananda
by Swami Kriyananda

This book presents a concept of God and spiritual meaning that will broadly appeal to everyone, from the most uncertain agnostic to the most fervent believer. Clearly and simply written, thoroughly non-sectarian and non-dogmatic in its approach, it is the perfect introduction to the spiritual path. Yogananda's core teachings are presented by his disciple, Swami Kriyananda.

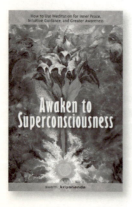

AWAKEN TO SUPERCONSCIOUSNESS

by Swami Kriyananda

This popular guide includes everything you need to know about the philosophy and practice of meditation, and how to apply the meditative mind to resolve common daily conflicts in uncommon, superconscious ways. Superconsciousness is the hidden mechanism at work behind intuition, spiritual and physical healing, successful problem solving, and finding deep and lasting joy.

THE ART & SCIENCE OF RAJA YOGA
by Swami Kriyananda

Contains fourteen lessons in which the original yoga science emerges in all its glory—a proven system for realizing one's spiritual destiny. This is the most comprehensive course available on yoga and meditation today. Over 450 pages of text and photos give you a complete and detailed presentation of yoga postures, yoga philosophy, affirmations, meditation instruction, and breathing techniques. Also included are suggestions for daily yoga routines, information on proper diet, recipes, and alternative healing techniques. The book also comes with an audio CD that contains: a guided yoga postures sessions, a guided meditation, and an inspiring talk on how you can use these techniques to solve many of the problems of daily life.

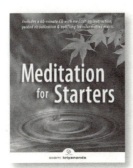

MEDITATION FOR STARTERS
by Swami Kriyananda

If you have wanted to learn to meditate, but never had a chance, this is the place to start. Filled with easy-to-follow instructions, beautiful guided visualizations, and answers to important questions on meditation, the book includes: what meditation is (and isn't); how to relax your body and prepare yourself for going within; and techniques for interiorizing and focusing the mind. Includes a 60-minute companion CD with guided visualization and meditation instruction.

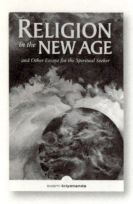

RELIGION IN THE NEW AGE

Swami Kriyananda

Our planet has entered an "Age of Energy" that will affect us for centuries to come. We can see evidence of this all around us: in ultra-fast computers, the quickening of communication and transportation, and the shrinking of time and space. This fascinating book of essays explores how this new age will change our lives, especially our spiritual seeking. Covers a wide range of upcoming societal shifts——in leadership, relationships, and self-development——including the movement away from organized religion to inner experience.

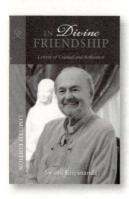

IN DIVINE FRIENDSHIP

Swami Kriyananda

This extraordinary book of nearly 250 letters, written over a thirty-year period by Swami Kriyananda, responds to practically any concern a spiritual seeker might have, such as: strengthening one's faith, accelerating one's spiritual progress, meditating more deeply, responding to illness, earning a living, attracting a mate, raising children, overcoming negative self-judgments, and responding to world upheavals.

Connecting all of these letters is the love, compassion, and wisdom of Swami Kriyananda, one of the leading spiritual figures of our time. The letters describe in detail his efforts to fulfill his Guru's commission to establish spiritual communities, and offer invaluable advice to leaders everywhere on how to avoid the temptations of materialism, selfishness, and pride. A spiritual treasure that speaks to truth seekers at all levels.

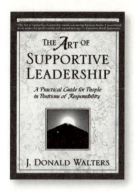

THE ART OF SUPPORTIVE LEADERSHIP

A Practical Guide for People in Positions of Responsibility
J. Donald Walters (Swami Kriyananda)

You can learn to be a more effective leader by viewing leadership in terms of shared accomplishments rather than personal advancement. Drawn from timeless Eastern wisdom, this book is clear, concise, and practical—designed from the start to produce results quickly and simply.

Used in training seminars in the U.S., Europe, and India, this book gives practical advice for leaders and potential leaders to help increase effectiveness, creativity, and team building. Individual entrepreneurs, corporations such as Kellogg, military and police personnel, and non-profit organizations are using this approach.

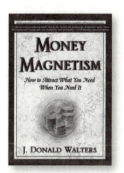

MONEY MAGNETISM

How to Attract What You Need When You Need It
J. Donald Walters (Swami Kriyananda)

This book can change your life by transforming how you think and feel about money. According to the author, anyone can attract wealth: "There need be no limits to the flow of your abundance." Through numerous true stories and examples, Swami Kriyananda vividly—sometimes humorously—shows you how and why the principles of money magnetism work, and how you can immediately start applying them to achieve greater success in your material and your spiritual life.

AUDIOBOOK AND MUSIC SELECTIONS

METAPHYSICAL MEDITATIONS
Swami Kriyananda

Kriyananda's soothing voice guides you in thirteen different meditations based on the soul-inspiring, mystical poetry of Paramhansa Yogananda. Each meditation is accompanied by beautiful classical music to help you quiet your thoughts and prepare for deep states of meditation. Includes a full recitation of Yogananda's poem "Samadhi," which appears in *Autobiography of a Yogi*. A great aid to the serious meditator, as well as to those just beginning their practice.

MEDITATIONS TO AWAKEN SUPERCONSCIOUSNESS
Guided Meditations on the Light
Swami Kriyananda

Featuring two beautiful guided meditations as well as an introductory section to help prepare the listener for meditation, this extraordinary recording of visualizations can be used either by itself, or as a companion to the book, *Awaken to Superconsciousness*. The soothing, transformative words, spoken over inspiring sitar background music, creates one of the most unique guided meditation products available.

RELAX: MEDITATIONS FOR FLUTE AND CELLO
Donald Walters
Featuring David Eby and Sharon Nani

This CD is specifically designed to slow respiration and heart rate, bringing listeners to their calm center. This recording features fifteen melodies for flute and cello, accompanied by harp, guitar, keyboard, and strings. Excellent for creating a calming atmosphere for work and home.

AUM: MANTRA OF ETERNITY

Swami Kriyananda

This recording features nearly seventy minutes of continuous vocal chanting of AUM, the Sanskrit word meaning peace and oneness of spirit. AUM, the cosmic creative vibration, is extensively discussed by Yogananda in *Autobiography of a Yogi*. Chanted here by his disciple, Kriyananda, this recording is a stirring way to tune into this cosmic power.

Other titles in the Mantra Series:

Gayatri Mantra*
Mahamrityanjaya Mantra*
Maha Mantra*

BLISS CHANTS

Ananda Kirtan

Chanting focuses and lifts the mind to higher states of consciousness. *Bliss Chants* features chants written by Yogananda and his direct disciple, Swami Kriyananda. They're performed by Ananda Kirtan, a group of singers and musicians from Ananda, one of the world's most respected yoga communities. Chanting is accompanied by guitar, harmonium, kirtals, and tabla.

Other titles in the Chant Series:

Divine Mother Chants	Power Chants
Love Chants	Peace Chants
Wisdom Chants*	Wellness Chants*

Visit our website to view all our available titles in books, audiobooks, spoken word, music and DVDs.

www.crystalclarity.com

* Coming Soon

CRYSTAL CLARITY PUBLISHERS

Crystal Clarity Publishers offers additional resources to assist you in your spiritual journey including many other books, a wide variety of inspirational and relaxation music composed by Swami Kriyananda, and yoga and meditation videos. To see a complete listing of our products, contact us for a print catalog or see our website: www.crystalclarity.com

Crystal Clarity Publishers

14618 Tyler Foote Rd., Nevada City, CA 95959

TOLL FREE: 800.424.1055 or 530.478.7600 / FAX: 530.478.7610

EMAIL: clarity@crystalclarity.com

ANANDA WORLDWIDE

Ananda Sangha, a worldwide organization founded by Swami Kriyananda, offers spiritual support and resources based on the teachings of Paramhansa Yogananda. There are Ananda spiritual communities in Nevada City, Sacramento, and Palo Alto, California; Seattle, Washington; Portland, Oregon; as well as a retreat center and European community in Assisi, Italy, and communities near New Delhi and Pune, India. Ananda supports more than 75 meditation groups worldwide.

For more information about Ananda Sangha
communities or meditation groups near you, please
call 530.478.7560 or visit www.ananda.org.

THE EXPANDING LIGHT

Ananda's guest retreat, The Expanding Light, offers a varied, year-round schedule of classes and workshops on yoga, meditation, and spiritual practice. You may also come for a relaxed personal renewal, participating in ongoing activities as much or as little as you wish. The beautiful serene mountain setting, supportive staff, and delicious vegetarian food provide an ideal environment for a truly meaningful, spiritual vacation.

For more information, please call 800.346.5350
or visit www.expandinglight.org.